LIFE STRATEGIES FOR PARENTING TEENAGERS 4-IN-1 COMBO PACK

POSITIVE PARENTING, TIPS AND UNDERSTANDING TEENS FOR

BUKKY EKINE-OGUNLANA

TCECPUBLISHING.COM

Published by

TCEC Publishing
TCEC House
14-18 Ada Street, London Fields,
E8 4QU, England, Great Britain.

CONTENTS

PARENTING TEENS IN A PANDEMIC

PARENTING TEEN BOYS IN TODAY'S CHALLENGING WORLD

PARENTING TEEN GIRLS IN TODAY'S CHALLENGING WORLD

LIFE STRATEGIES FOR
TEENAGERS

*This book is dedicated to our three amazing children
and all the beautiful children all over the world who
over the years have passed through the T.C.E.C 6-16
years programme. Thank you for the opportunity to
serve you and invest in your colourful and bright future.*

PARENTING TEENS IN A PANDEMIC

PROVEN METHODS FOR IMPROVING TEENAGERS BEHAVIOUR WITH WHOLE BRAIN TRAINING

INTRODUCTION

Raising your teenager seems like a Herculean task from the get-go as teenagers are often synonymous with mood-swings and rebellious behavior. Puberty is one of the stages in a child's life that brings forth anxiety and insecurity within parents as teenagers face puberty and the changes that accompany it. At this stage in your teen's life, they are experiencing extreme emotions and grappling with new sensations and changes and most choose to retreat as far away from their parents as possible, both emotionally and physically. But parents were once teenagers as well, and while we may not have all the answers, we can certainly sympathize with the plights teenagers face and try to support them to the best of our ability during this difficult time. This book seeks to rid the negative connotation surrounding raising adolescents and the reputation it has garnered for being notoriously difficult. Raising your teenager successfully starts with you, the parent, and this tenet will be reiterated throughout this book.

As your teenager is moving towards greater independence and making their own choices in life, the challenge is for you to find a happy medium and balance to guide your teens. This, however, can all completely fall apart in the face of a global pandemic. With most teens cooped up indoors with the rest of their family, development and behaviors have been severely affected by the lack of social interaction that your teen has grown accustomed to. The stress and pressure have been doubly difficult for both parents and children who attempt to navigate their way through discipline and imparting lessons, all while being confined to the family home.

This book provides tips and tricks to raising your teens in the midst of a global shutdown. With plenty of families on lockdown and spending more time indoors than ever, the problems that have arisen from raising your teens can be immense or minor. Every teenager is different, just like every parent is different and the environment you are raising your child in will differ from household to household. This book seeks to address the concerns that may crop up in adolescence on the ever-changing and unpredictable landscape of a global pandemic.

KNOWING WHEN YOUR TEEN IS GOING THROUGH CHANGES

*P*uberty entails changing tides and newfound challenges for your teen. The question parents seem to ask when faced with this is "How do I know if my child is experiencing the changes associated with becoming a teen?" What every parent should bear in mind is that every teen is completely different. They are molded by the different circumstances of your life and there is never one tried and tested way to raise teens into fully-fledged adults. However, there are a few things that you may try to identify what your teen is going through.

Establishing respect begins at the early stages of your child's life. From a young age, your child should be taught that humans around them have the same capacity to experience the same extreme emotions that they feel, which is why we have to treat others with respect and kindness. Valuing respect in your household branches out into a myriad of benefits. Your child will learn to listen to others and mitigate their own extreme feelings, which will greatly aid them during their teenage years.

There is no denying that adolescence is a turbulent time for children. Many lash out on their siblings and parents because it can be an incredibly awkward time for them. At the same time, from a parent's perspective, this time is crucial for setting them up for adulthood and is considered to be their formative years. It is incredibly important to develop these good habits from a young age, before they are met with the challenges and tests of puberty as they experience physical changes and their mental health can be affected by this immensely.

For plenty of other teens, this scary time can lead them to completely shut out the people around them. You may find yourself growing increasingly distant with your teen without a reason to pinpoint why. Some teens react by clinging onto their parents, afraid of new social inter-actions and new forms of anxiety develop. Some chil-dren might appear to have hardly any reaction to the changes their bodies are going through.

Regardless of how your child reacts, it would be utterly remiss to simply brush their time as an adolescent off. This is not a vacation time for parents. While raising a teen means a lesser need to constantly monitor them, it poses its own set of new challenges that you have to prepare and that parents have yet to experience when raising their kids from infants to young children. Parents know to prioritize their children, but this can mean a lot of different things as teens are diverse all around. For some parents, this can mean sitting them down for a heart to heart and discussing the changes they may be experiencing and broaching on the subject of their mental health. Some parents require professional help by seeking out therapy for your children. Ultimately, it comes down to you being perceptive to your children and how their behaviors may be changing. As they enter into teenagerhood, anticipate that your children will be going through some big changes, whether they react extremely or not. Puberty will always happen and will always be a natural part of a child's life as they age and mature. As the parent, it is your responsibility to be proactive and figure out what exactly your teen is going through in order for you to move ahead with strategies to manage everything healthily and successfully.

Factoring in a global pandemic, raising children has had to go through its own evolution as parents are now at home more than ever. Take advantage of the fact that you are around your children all day long. While you may be occupied with working from home, and your children may be spending their time with their online schooling, your proximity to your kids is not to take for granted. Take this chance to observe your children closely without hovering over them to notice any changes in their behavior, discomfort or habits. Another great way is to be proactive and reach out to your child's teachers and request updates on how your child is handling the various responsibilities and the transition to online school. While teachers aren't able to necessarily build the same relationship with their students that a classroom fosters, understanding their quality of academic work can be an indication of how they are coping with the changes and transitions of online education.

During this time, you can see how your teen conducts themselves on a regular basis and responds to various stressors like school or siblings in order to determine if your child is experiencing difficulty settling into teenagerhood and the new responsibilities and developments it brings.

Your free gift!

AS A WAY OF SAYING THANK YOU
FOR
PURCHASING THIS BOOK, I AM
OFFERING YOU A FREE GIFT AT THE
END OF THE BOOK

MATURITY

Once you have established that your child is maturing, as a parent, this means increased responsibilities that come hand in hand with more freedoms that they will expect you to afford them with. Raising toddlers will look like child's play when you realize what you are up against.

Teens expect a myriad of new freedoms as they age; an increased curfew, more allowance, an independence over their own schoolwork, etc. A time of maturity means that teens are more opinionated and express themselves in a multitude of ways. But as the parent, what will always remain constant are the basic values that you would have established from a young age; like compassion, respect, kindness, empathy, honesty and a multitude of others to shape your children into good people. Parents set the example for their children and have to be conscious of the fact that their behaviour will be mimicked at some point or another by their kids. Establish with your children that just because they may be older and somewhat wiser, they are still expected to act accordingly as they have been raised. As the parent, holding these values steadfast in the household is crucial because your teens might be more tempted to act out as they are older and oftentimes have a surge of confidence that leads them to undermine your authority. Ultimately, this becomes your chance to re-establish discipline in your household, but in a way that is appropriate and effective for teens.

Now is your chance to educate your children on accountability. As you age, the mistakes you make have increasingly drastic consequences and putting these good values and habits into practice is crucial as your child independently branches out on their own and engages in new social situations and meet new people. Make sure that your teen is aware of what maturity means in terms of how people regard them as independent, and the fact that you won't always be around to take responsibility for them. As they grow up, they are expected to keep their word and follow through with their own promises. While parents still have to take responsibility for their children, teenagers will attest to how you have raised them as they start to enter into the real world and face real-life situations.

For most parents, as their teens mature, good behavior is rewarded with more freedoms and choices. So, when the time comes for disciplining their teens, they choose to take away privileges like computers or gaming systems if they are unable to handle their newfound freedom responsibly and appropriately. Setting new boundaries that are clear and strictly adhered to is crucial. Never assume that the same rules will apply to your child as the grow and evolve as people. Your teen may be obsessed with computers one day but be completely into their cellphones the next. Keep up with your children as now that they are older, adolescence is the age where kids begin outsmarting their parents and finding more creative and inventive ways to get out of punishments and discipline. It takes evaluating your child and being proactive in order to learn the best away to take away their privileges. Leveraging their cellphones for good behavior encourages them to be more mindful of their attitudes and the values that you have instilled within them.

As you navigate through the pandemic with your teen, part of their journey of maturing is to ensure that they are just as informed about the goings on of the real world.

How to Inform Your Teens About the Coronavirus:

- Keep in mind that since teenagers are more apt with technology and are potentially just as informed as you expect them to be.
- This is not your time to sugar coat things for them. Bear in mind the realities of the situation and inform them of the bleak circumstances in the world.
- Remain calm as you do so and always remember that your teenagers will pick up your energy and might potentially recreate it.
- Reassure them of their safety and stress the importance of taking proper precautions.
- Express that wearing masks and staying away from their social circle and school is the best way to keep everyone safe and prevent the spread of the virus.
- Make yourself available to them to answer questions and acknowledge their fears and stress.
- While you may encourage them to stay informed with ongoing news and updates, too much information can often have detrimental effects on their mental health.
- Anxiety may result from having such serious conversations from both parent or teen, so be prepared to manage and cope in a healthy way.
- Inform them about the misinformation that may

be available and encourage them to use trusted medical sources to form their opinions about COVID-19.

- Lastly, educate your teenagers on the proper procedures to keep them and their family safe. Proper hand washing techniques and sanitization habits are a must.

PEERS

*P*art of the challenge for parents when it comes to raising teens is accepting that you are no longer the greatest influence on your child's life any longer. Instead, this is where their peers come in. Their friends and other cohort usually around their age will relate more to their struggles and changes in a way that you simply will not be able to replace. As a parent, understand this can be a difficult thing to come to terms with, but part of maturing is gaining their own experiences. While we can hope that these experiences are positive, sometimes they can be quite negative at the same time.

The influence of your child's peers can certainly be positive. It can result to your teen feeling more reassured or confident as they see their own friends performing in such a way. Sometimes, peer influence can manifest in the form of how your child dresses or even working harder at school. Considering the number of people your child will meet through school and extracurricular activities, their peers can have a positive experience on their development.

However, in that same regard, when your child enters teenagerhood, the term "peer pressure" is often thrown around. At this age, children who are entering this stage of their lives have the challenge of facing a number of social situations where they are subject to the pressure that will shake the foundations of what you have built and taught them. The voice of reason in your child can fly out the window when faced with doing what everyone else is doing. This can manifest in changes in the way they speak, TV shows that they watch or indeed, the pressure of drugs and alcohol poses as a hurdle at a young age.

Parents struggle with this as they want to be accepting but fear that their teens will make mistakes and bad decisions. The question that parents constantly ask is "How do I compete with my teens cohort of friends?" Firstly, understand that you are their parents and ultimately, you call the shots when it comes to your child's life. From an early age, your child sees you as an authority figure. Their peers aren't a group that you should aspire to compete with. Instead, this is the opportunity for you to re-establish your authority as a parent while also relinquishing your hold on your kids. As they enter into the stage of adolescence, they may choose to rebel and go against your values but understand that this is your chance to talk to them and evaluate their behavior. This is your teen's way of testing the boundaries.

Secondly, your child is trying to find their place in the world. This will entail experimentation and trying new things. You should prepare for this early on by shaping their values from a young age. As they grow and face more stressors and pressure, the more your child is happy with who they are and having a sense of security prevents that from making poor decisions that will greatly affect them in the long run. It's normal to worry that your child is making poor decisions and risking the values that you have instilled in them in order to fit in with their friends. But coping with these pressures is where you come in as a parent. Instilling a sense of security in their own convictions is how to get your children out of these situations. You have to trust them from making the bad decisions by teaching them why certain things can be poor choices and what the consequences can potentially be. In the case of underage drinking for example, teens are especially excited to experience the new world of alcohol. Educate your children on the laws surrounding drinking in your country and how it can affect them negatively. Tell them about the consequences they face should they be caught by the police, reiterating that as much as you would want to help them out of these situations, sometimes it simply is not in your own hands solely.

How to Cope with Peer Pressure:

- Establish security with your child and bring them up with confidence and encourage them for a high esteem. They should feel confident in themselves to know when to make the right decisions. Therefore, when faced with situations that they are uncomfortable in, they know the right course of action.
- Communicate with your child. Reassure them that you are here to listen without judgement, and that they can be themselves. Allow them to see that they can place their trust in adults.
- Suggest ways to say no. Your child may feel intimidated to say no in situations that make them uncomfortable but instill in them that the word "no" holds a lot of power and that they have every right to express when they are uncomfortable with something.
- Give your teens a way out of uncomfortable situations. Whether it's telling them to call your or text you so that you will be there to pick

them its up or being with friends that they can trust who will support their decisions.

- Its important for you to respond to these situations without judgement. Rather than focusing on the fact that your child may have been on the cusp of making a poor decision, focus on the fact that they reached out to you so that you can establish that you are the right person to call should they ever need assistance.

- Encourage your children to spend time with a variety of peers. Sometimes as a parent, you may see certain friends as a good influence, but this may not be the case when it comes down to the relationship your child shares with them. If your child chooses not to divulge the details of all of their relationships, try to instead encourage them to meet with various friends from school extracurricular activities or even your neighbours. If a friendship goes poorly in one aspect, they will always have others to fall back on.

There are certain cases that are tell-tale signs that point towards when you should be worried about negative peer pressure affecting your children. If your child seems to be in a negative mood for long periods of time, negative peer pressure that even go so far as bullying could be the reason for it.

Signs Your Child is Experiencing Difficulty:

- Constant feelings of hopelessness and low moods that are persistent even when your child is doing their favorite activities
- Antisocial behavior or a refusal to participate in any social situations, especially if this behavior differs from how your child usually acts
- Sudden changes in behavior without an immediate cause that you can pinpoint
- Sleeping for extended periods of time or not sleeping at all
- Loss of appetite or reliance on food to cope with their emotions
- Withdrawal from activities they used to enjoy and any interactions with family or friends
- Negative statements that indicate a loss of will to live or motivation

These signs can be indicative of your child experiencing some difficult times with their mental health. If you spot any of these or have any concerns, the best course of action is to speak to your child and try to form an understanding of what they are facing. Allow them to lean on you and trust you as they tell you the difficulties in their life. This does not mean punishing them immediately for making a poor decision, if they are the immediate cause of this. Instead, focus on what they are going through and express to them that there will always be a way to cope with their pain healthily and that you will support them through their road to recovering from these hard times.

The next step after this may be to consult a professional if your child is facing greater challenges that you simply may not be qualified to help manage. Understand that this is completely okay. You are not lesser of a parent for wanting to reach out to a professional for help. In fact, you are even more so a responsible parent for wanting the best treatments for helping your child deal with the challenges they are faced with. Professionals like child therapists and psychologists have the means and resources to accurately identify the issue your child is facing and come up with the appropriate means of coping with these issues.

One parent in particular had experienced her daughter completely shutting out her family and friends, choosing to stay in her room for hours on end without interacting with the rest of her family. At first, the parent attributed it to online school and the fact that her child might have been struggling to cope with the transition from physically going to school and the anxieties of the pandemic.

At fourteen years old, this can be a difficult time and their way of coping is to shut themselves away from their family. However, the parent soon realized that this was not the case and the child was going through some more substantial and difficult times. The parent immediately sought to understand what was going on and since they had a strong relationship, the child ended up telling her parent that she was experiencing extreme anxiety from the pressures brought on in school. Through conversations and spending time together, the parent realized the scope of the child's issue and chose to rely on a professional, who then provided healthy coping methods for the child experiencing anxiety. The parent relinquished their overprotectiveness over their child and chose to step back, serving as a support system as she faced her demons through professional help. While the journey has been long and a constant work in progress, the daughter has been slowly and steadily improving by identifying her triggers and having a healthy way of coping, as well as a constant pillar of support through her parent.

Just like this parent, know when it is your time to relinquish your hold on your children. As much as you want to be their constant pillar of strength and as much as you want them to rely on you, they will most definitely have to rely on other people for support as well. This does not mean that you are any less important, but it does mean that you bear the responsibility of making the transition as seamless as possible for your child. Refusing to let them go creates another set of problems for your child. Part of parenting is putting another person first, before yourself. In this case, as difficult as it may be to accept that you cannot fix all of your teen's problems, put them first and respect their decision to develop their own terms as they age and grow up.

A Note About Professionals:

Professional help comes in a number of different ways. No two children are the exact same, which means that there is not a single cure for every single problem. Understand that "curing" your child of anxiety or depression is a dangerous way to look at things. Rather than "curing" your children, professional help serves to aid your children in mitigating their emotions and finding healthy coping mechanisms.

Remember that all therapists are different. You may find that sometimes your child does not click as well with whoever they are speaking to and this is not an issue. It may take some time to find the right person to fit your child's needs. If you don't have the luxury or money to shop around, consider trying online resources. There are plenty of safe websites to provide counselling for your children. Every child's mental health varies in degree. In order to cope with extreme feelings, trying out online counselling might be a good way to identify what your child is going through or find a neutral party to be a non-judgemental ear for your children to speak to that is cost efficient and convenient, especially during the time of a pandemic. It can be a good starting point for you to determine if you need to take things further by consulting with your doctor.

YOUR ROLE

*A*s previously mentioned, one of the biggest challenges parents face during this time is learning when to let go of their children and afford them with independence in order to allow them to find themselves and discover who they are. The teenage years are crucial for this very reason. While their children experience growth, parents struggle to evolve alongside them as they are so used to being their child's primary decision makers throughout their younger years. Many make the mistake of not relinquishing their control over their children which can lead to disastrous effects as they become at odds with each other as children resent their parents for their overcontrolling nature while parents are frustrated constantly because their child refuses to listen to them.

Finding that balance is key. But parents are not sure of how to go about finding that sweet spot of guiding their children while being an authority figure while also simultaneously being a friend to their child and a figure that they can trust.

1. Step up to the role of being a coach, rather than a dictator.

When your children are young, you dictate every aspect of their lives; from what time they eat, what time they sleep, what they watch, etc. Being a parent to a younger child requires constant supervision that parents develop almost robotically as every day is a new day of routines and keeping things constant. As your child ages, this routine loosens up and your teen is the extreme end of this as they begin making their own decisions.

Rather than treating your teen as another stage in their life to control and monitor as you did when they were younger, step down from this role and allow them to control aspects of their lives. When kids reach adolescence, they need to prepare for adulthood in a way that means making their own decisions and being able to justify them on their own terms. For parents, this means fostering this need to be independent. Forcing your children to follow your schedule every single day and dictating every part of their lives will eventually lead to them defying you the first chance they get.

This by no means entails that parents become disengaged and any less involved in their child's life. It simply means that by adolescence, our focus shifts and we hand the reins over to our kids to dictate the course of their lives. This also means plenty of mistakes will be made, and there is nothing wrong with this. Your job here is to guide them and provide them with the emotional support that they need to get through the challenges life presents them.

2. Influence

Your children are no longer small, nor do they soak up your every word like in a way that they used to. The now have an understanding that your way of living life is not the only way to do things. Your kids will argue and have a differing view from. Parents often feel helpless when they have especially argumentative kids as they feel like they're simply not getting through to them. But just like they were when they were young, actions speak louder than words and the way parents carry themselves can have a huge impact on how your child will in turn carry their selves. Your influence now has to evolve along with your kids. Because they have an inherent yearn to be autonomous, simply telling them what to do won't always work and can lead to even more arguments and dissent between the two of you. Instead, treat them like an adult. Talk to them like you would with your own peers. They want to be able to feel like an adult in the situation, rather than a dynamic that makes them feel lesser than.

3. Things are going to seem difficult

As soon as puberty hits, a string of uncertainties come along that your children face and more often than not will not approach you for advice or support. In order to really provide the support that your child needs, you will have to discuss uncomfortable topics with them. Talking to teenagers about their lives can be an extremely daunting task but a great way to get started is to let your teens lead the way. Bring up a difficult topic and get them to elaborate. The job of the parent here is to be observant and listen to what they are saying. These little conversations can often be the pathway leading to discussing big and difficult conversations that you may both be dreading but are equally as important for parents and their kids to have.

Topics You May Need to Discuss with Your Teen

- Mental health awareness: Prioritize your child's mental health just as you prioritize their physical health. Discussing anxiety and depression can be a nerve-wracking thing, but doing so let's your children know that you care and support them no matter what they are facing

- Sexual activity: Later in a teen's years, they may start having boyfriends or girlfriends, which can lead to engaging in sexual activity. Be open to what your children discusses with you.

- Sexual and gender identity: At some point in time, your teens may question their sexual identity. Listen to them to be able to give the right answers to their questions and educate yourself on what identity can mean for a teen.

- Alcohol and drugs: Be open and honest with your teens as you educate them on alcohol and drugs. You want to be able to trust them to make the right decisions if they are ever faced with the temptation, especially when they are underage. Inform them about substance abuse and how it can destroy their lives. Encourage them to be responsible and it is crucial to build a strong foundation so that they can be open with you about their experiences with alcohol and drugs.

- Internet safety: Social media and the internet are a huge part of most teenagers' lives. It plays a massive impact on molding adolescence and teens can often get so caught up on the latest internet trends. Impart on them safe procedures online, like withholding personal information and protecting their identity. Furthermore, it is important to reiterate that social media is extremely superficial. Social media can have a negative impact on your child's self-esteem and confidence, so having a healthy relationship with Instagram, Facebook and Twitter are important to develop.

- Saying 'no': It is extremely crucial that parents instill within their children the ability to say 'no'. It can be the mitigating factor in getting them out of uncomfortable or dangerous situations. Teach your children to be confident in themselves by reiterating that if they are ever uncomfortable, they have every right to say 'no' and get out of the situation. This is incredibly important for teens to learn, especially as they are increasingly exposed to substances and even people that may be less than savory as they gain their own independence.

STRATEGIES DURING THE PANDEMIC

*C*oping during a worldwide pandemic is understandably difficult for both parents and children alike. This time is incredibly anxiety inducing as you worry about avoiding the virus and ensuring your family is safe while trying to maintain some semblance of normalcy as you spend an increased amount of time at home. Parents are extremely worried during this time and understandably so, as there seems to be plenty of negativity going on in the world. For you to put on a positive front at all times is simply not realistic, but there are some strategies and strides you can make to improve the quality of life while everyone is cooped up at home.

1. Set a routine

Your teen may be old enough to have their own routine and that's perfectly acceptable. Especially when factoring in online school and your own work hours, creating a set routine for teens differs from creating a routine for young children who require a routine in order to have a productive day. A great way to establish a routine is by having set mealtimes with family like breakfast and dinners. These times are especially great because it's a great way to set up your day with positivity in the mornings and by dinner time in the evening, you can spend it reflecting on how your day went with the rest of your family.

2. Spend time together

With so many hours of the day being spent in front of screens and virtually meeting people, spending time together after work is a no-brainer here. Having real life, physical social interactions helps your children mentally and encourages them to not take their own family for granted. Watching a movie together, playing board games, or even cooking dinner together are great ways to get your child involved and keep their brains alert and stimulated and engaged in their surroundings, rather than maintaining their focus simply on their computers for days on end.

3. Go outside

While travelling and going to enclosed public spaces are activities that are discouraged, there are still plenty of things to do in the outdoors that are safe and free. Go outside and explore your neighbourhood by going on walks or jogs to give your teen an opportunity to exercise their legs and get their cardiovascular health going. Consider turning this into a family activity or perhaps just one-on-one time with your teen to take the opportunity to get to know them better and learn how they are doing mentally in terms of dealing with this difficult time.

4. Exercising

As the previous point discussed jogging and cardiovascular health, exercise is a crucial way to help your teens cope with the pandemic. It's a healthy way to channel all of their pent-up energy into and can be fun for the whole family, or only for the individual. There are plenty of online resources that provide free and fun ways to get your body moving. YouTube is a fantastic resource for this as it features plenty of content creators with fun choreography to dance to or great workout videos your teen can do. Again, consider joining them. This is a great way to focus on your own mental health as well as parents are just as human and may be experiencing some difficulty during this time. The benefits for exercise are numerous and for a lot of people, have been a saving grace during these unprecedented times.

5. Encourage them to take up a new hobby

There are plenty of pursuits outside of computers and TV. Encourage your children to explore a hobby that is offline like reading, writing, art, or even cooking. These are great ways to get your teens engaged in something healthy and gives them the ability to create and imagine. It's a great way to spend their afternoons away from screens and focusing on the virtual world.

PLEASE LEAVE A 1-CLICK REVIEW!

I hope you enjoyed reading this book!

If you haven't done so yet, I would be incredibly thankful if you could take 60 seconds to write a brief review on Amazon or the platform of purchase , even if it's just a few sentences!

Your feedback will be a huge help in helping other readers benefit from the information in the book.

You can also contact us by sending an email to tcecpublishing@outlook.com

Like us on https://www.facebook.com/tcecpublishing/

Join our Facebookpagehttps://www.facebook.com/groups/397683731371863/ to stay updated on our next releases!

See you there!

CONCLUSION

Now that you have some tips and tricks in mind, go out there and use them. Remember that the pandemic is an anxiety-inducing time for everyone, parents included. As a means of coping, we have to stay calm for the sake of our teens' development and for their own mental health as well. The biggest takeaway from this book is to bear in mind that your children are humans too. They are going through a doubly hard time as they face the challenges of adolescence without being surrounded by their friends in the midst of a pandemic, which for teens can be extremely devastating. While you may not be able to completely replace their friends, parents can represent a safe space for their children to share their biggest problems with. You can certainly fill a void as you provide a source of support for your teens during these trying times.

PARENTING TEEN BOYS IN TODAY'S CHALLENGING WORLD

PROVEN METHODS FOR IMPROVING TEENAGERS BEHAVIOUR WITH WHOLE BRAIN TRAINING

INTRODUCTION

Parenting has undeniably evolved over the years. With the rise of technology and social media, these aspects have greatly impacted how we raise our children as we are exposed to new, creative, and unique ways to parent our children. These have had incredible benefits for parents around the world as we navigate through the challenges that are presented through parenting with a community of other parents for support and encouragement. On the downside however, it presents a number of avenues for you to take as a parent to raise your child that can be overwhelming, confusing and doubly daunting.

While there is no "one size fits all" approach to parenting, nor is there a single formula that will apply to every single child, there are cardinal rules that are encouraged, especially throughout the course of this book and its companion book that is geared specifically towards raising teen girls. Along every stage within your child's life, one of the main cardinal rules is for you, the parent, to evolve alongside your children. You simply would not apply the same parenting techniques on a toddler onto your teenager, as much your teenager may sometimes test your patience like a toddler would. While your children mature and face new social situations and experience the myriad of new emotions that life presents them, they in turn experience a personal growth of their own that parents have to grapple with quickly in order to develop their parenting techniques alongside them. This often poses as a challenge for parents around the world because as much as parenting means adopting the role of a guide to steer your child through the various challenges that life presents, it also means going through a form of growth yourself, a notion that is quite often neglected when it comes to discussing parenting.

Growth as an adult is often an overlooked notion, because adults are seen as seemingly all-knowing and prepared for the world that is ahead of them. Ultimately, growth and evolution are sure ways to not only develop as an adult, but to also show your children that life is a constant series of tests of your strength and courage. Parents often fall into the trap of posing as an authoritative dictator-type figure in their child's life by being overly strict or adopting a "helicopter parent" style. Or the opposite can occur, where parents are simply too laid-back and hands off when it comes to raising their children. Sometimes this can unintentional, or a consequence of parents attempting to navigate through the endless decisions they have to make for their kids. Many parents start out this way, but the most important part is that they choose to evolve. They acknowledge the mistakes they are making and choose to grow and learn from them. This is the biggest lesson to take out of this book. You may apply the techniques and strategies presented in this book closely and strictly yet find that your child is not responding accordingly. The next step is to try another method and continue adapting and learning from this process. This is the single greatest tip that we can impart onto parents, which is that parenting is a process and takes time and growth.

Making mistakes while parenting will always happen as you attempt to raise your children to become good citizens of society. This is inevitable and many parents grapple with this, even if their children are older and they have been parenting for years. The fear of mistakes often hold parents back which in turn can hinder your child's development. It is an incredibly difficult and scary feat for adults who have children, as bearing this responsibility is no small task. Most parents are determined to raise their children to the best of their ability and present them with all of the opportunities to grow and develop from fledglings into fully-grown adults. With that intent, they are faced with the question of *how* exactly to go about this. This book is a response to this very question.

Seasoned parents would argue that teenagerhood is the most difficult time for parenting. Many parents might say that this time period for your teenagers is a time of high emotions and added pressure as your teenager experience leaving their childhood and are on the cusp of adulthood. Your teens are in the process of making big decisions that will affect their futures, particularly with their educations and careers which is an incredibly stressful time for most. Teens could be experiencing more complex relationships and the emotions associated with that. Additionally, as your children age, they become more accustomed to the fact that the world is more flawed than what they might have been used to during their protected childhood years that featured a far more idealistic and positive view. As your children age, they are met with the responsibilities that they will have to take on as adults. With all of these in mind, the immense stress that can weigh on a teen's mental health during this time can be immense. With this transition of age being so formative and crucial for your teens, the same stress and pressure reflects onto parents as well, which is why teenagerhood is seen as a particularly difficult time for both parents and children alike.

Yet these years also bring a number of new joys. As your children are now aging, they are grasping a better understanding of adulthood which means that they are able to more accurately empathize with their parents and build a new facet to the parent and child dynamic as they form their own opinions and experience the world differently but are able to articulate and share their thoughts with you. This aspect is a joy for many parents, as they are able to really develop a friendship and a deeper respect for their children as they view them in the different light that maturity brings. Parents often find that they are able to share more with their children at this age, which is crucial for fostering a healthy relationship. Like most things, teenagerhood has its own set of positives and qualms for both parents and teens alike.

The most crucial point that will consistently be reiterated is that no two children are the same. Every child experiences their surrounding environment differently and has their own notions of the world they are raised in. Likewise, all children perceive themselves differently and it is extremely crucial that parents respect this. These books are framed through gender, with the first part being catered to raising teen girls, while the second part is geared towards raising teen boys. Understand that gender stereotypes can be extremely harmful to children. There is no right way to "act like a boy" or "act like a girl". These are incredibly dangerous ideas that parents must avoid when raising their children because it fosters limitations on your children simply because of their gender. While there are rules that exist in society, what also exist simultaneously is fluidity. The concept of gender is a slippery slope but ultimately, it is up to parents to lay a strong groundwork and foundation to build confidence within their children to accept themselves despite societal expectations. It is up to parents to teach their children that what they may like or dislike is simply a result of their preferences, and not a weakness. For example, if your son dislikes sports, it does not make him any less of a boy, let alone a man.

The parts of this book are divided by gender to play on the multi-dimensionality that is gender roles. Gender roles are an incredibly complex and intricate social conceptualization as it deems a range of behaviours that are attributed and desirable based on a person's sex. This way of thinking can be dangerous and certainly place limitations on your children. As much as we discourage gender stereotyping, there are a few inherent differences between boys and girls that should be differentiated and discussed when raising girls and boys. However, keep in mind that all of the tips are interchangeable between genders and can be applied to any child as they have no prerequisites or preconditions that need to be followed before being applied. These tips are universally applicable and really serve to nurture your teen's interests and needs, regardless of their gender.

hen raising teen boys and teen girls, there are some fundamental differences that exist. Some of these differences begin within the household, where boys are given less affection than their girl counterparts or allowing aggression and violent play by relying on the mantra of "boys will be boys". This is a slippery slope, as these notions that are seemingly innocent at the time can fester and develop into full psychological roadblocks that your children will have to face in their adulthood. These differences between genders are further fostered when your child enters the education system, particularly seen through the many education systems choose to segregate boys and girls during physical education classes. While education systems differ all around the world, the school system is often where these notions of gender and the applicable stereotypes are established with your child. By the time your child has entered their teen years, ideas of "running like a girl" or "acting like a boy" have firmly wormed their way into their mindset. It is an inevitable result of the education system.

What becomes key here is how parents pick up on what your child is learning and either nip these ideas in the bud or turn them into learning lessons for your children to show them a different scope that exists in the world. By doing so, you are setting your child up to be prepared for a world of diversity. You are also teaching them the incredibly important life lessons by imparting that they are simply not limited to the conditions of their gender.

Here are some techniques to employ to gather an understanding of how your teen boy may perceive themselves. This is the first step to deciphering how you might want to raise your teen boy and the techniques you want to employ to foster their interests.

1. Have a strong foundation

Having a relationship with your children is incredibly important and this is a known fact for every parent. A prerequisite to be able to even begin to help your children deal with the number of things they are facing through their teenage years is to have a strong foundation and a shared respect between each other. With the teen years being so divisive and stress filled, being able to face these challenges with parents by their side is incredibly crucial for teens. Similarly, knowing when your children are going through hard times or may be at crossroads really begins with a strong relationship that allows open communication and provides a safe space.

2. Be perceptive

Being proactive in your child's education and being aware of what they are being taught in their education is extremely important. For many parents, this may be a no-brainer, while some parents naively leave their children's education completely in the hands of their teachers. While teachers are incredibly vital and provide an insurmountable amount of support during your children's most formative years, playing a role in your child's education is equally just as important. Developing a relationship with your child's teacher and keeping tabs on where they are thriving academically can help greatly when it comes to tailoring your techniques of parenting towards them. Additionally, teachers are a great source for understanding how your teen may be doing socially and mentally, which in turn will provide next steps that may need to be taken in order to provide the support and help they need.

3. Be affectionate

Particularly in the case of boys, many parents make the mistake of feeding their daughters more affection than their sons for reasons in the realm of wanting to foster a sense of masculinity from a young age. This idea of affection and masculinity being tied is extremely problematic and can lead to plenty of issues down the line. Masculinity and affection are not tied together, and boys deserve as much love and affection that girls receive in their lifetime. Demonstrating warmth and affection to all your children equally, regardless of gender, allows them to do the same for their own children and avoid some of the issues that can arise out of not experiencing love from parental figures.

4. Avoid the "boys will be boys" mentality

This dangerous mentality is often used as an excuse to brush off certain behaviours or attitudes seen in boys. This is a slippery slope as it can foster violent tendencies and aggression that parents encourage as male behavior. It allows unconscious biases to form and allows boys to have a different framework of acceptable behaviours and attitudes that differs from girls. In other words, it gives them an excuse to engage in what could perhaps be inappropriate or unacceptable behaviour in the future. Using this phrase simply brushes off these impulses and is often used in specific cases of bullying which can be extremely harmful as it does not teach children that their actions are wrong and completely unacceptable. Instead, it gives them an excuse and a way out of facing real consequences and learning from their mistakes.

5. Be present

As much as your teenage son is growing up and becoming more and more mature every single day, while parents are expected to loosen the reins, it by no means entails completely abandoning parenting all together. You represent a guide for your child to follow and model after, even into their adult lives. Being present in their lives means continuing the relationship and bond you share, even if you may feel like they simply do not need you anymore. This is hardly ever the case when parents are evolving and growing alongside their children. Parents are able to simultaneously allow their children to flourish on their own terms while having a constant presence in their lives. This comes down to finding a balance and respecting the boundaries that your child imposes. While you may not like it at first, part of the process of being a parent is accepting hard to swallow pills like this and understanding that there will come a time where you will feel unwanted, but that certainly is not the case or the intention. What this really means is your children are growing up and becoming adults themselves.

6. Nurture self-expression

Limiting your sons to only express themselves within a framework of masculinity greatly hinders their development and can put your relationship with them in jeopardy. Rather than encouraging rigid binaries of masculinity and femininity, allow your children to gravitate towards their own likes and dislikes. These can manifest in a number of ways, from hobbies to the relationships they have. The important aspect of this is to always keep in mind to nurture these habits by showing your own support and respect towards your child's ways of self-expression, regardless of how it may manifest while you watch to know how to help. Every child grows and develops differently, so expecting your child to be just like your neighbour's son not only places unnecessary pressure on your son, but also sets yourself up for failure and disappointment. Rather than encouraging your child to emulate other people, allow your son to come into their own and become their own person. It largely lies on parents to foster this sense of self-confidence and respect of their own self. As your child ages, they will be more accustomed and open with who they are, and thus more willing to share with you what they are experiencing mentally, emotionally and socially as their parents.

7. Foster emotionality

Boys are often encouraged to not show their emotions, so much so that the stereotype is that girls are more emotional than boys. While this is a huge generalization, there is some truth to it and we may consider why this is the case. The reason for this lies in the fact that boys are simply told to put on a façade of rigidity and strength, where crying is now seen as a weakness. This, aside from being completely false, is dangerous as it encourages boys to bottle up their emotions which can lead to them spilling out in the most dangerous of situations. Rather than encourage your children to put on a brave face all the time, allow your boys to cry and experience the relief of dispelling their emotions in this way. Crying can be a healthier coping mechanism that can prevent your teens from turning to drugs or alcohol as a coping mechanism. The important part is to talk to your children after the fact and try to work out the extreme emotions they may be feeling. This has the greatest impact on your teens as they develop an understanding that their parents will always be a constant beacon of support.

8. Be a guide

Your children look to you as their role model from the minute they are brought into this world. This is simply what parenting is. But as they age, and especially by their teen years, inevitably your children will have more influences and face other figures who will greatly impact their lives. Respect this aspect, but also never relinquish your role as a guide to your children because ultimately you are still their parents. Always model behaviours that you yourself are proud of and respect because your children will model the same after you, whether consciously or not. Knowing that you have set your own standards for behaviours and attitudes in your household is a great way to find anomalies and notice how your child may be negatively influenced.

9. Family

The family dynamic can greatly benefit parenting your children because every person plays an important role in raising a teen. We have all heard of the African proverb "It takes a village to raise a child" and this certainly rings true when it comes to helping your children thrive and be the best that they can possibly be. Parents and siblings of an individual play their own roles in positively impacting an individual's life, so when it comes to understanding what your teen may be going through, relying on the different dynamics that may exist in your household is a way to ease some of the pressure a single parent may be experiencing. Siblings can tap into a different side of your struggling kid in a way that parents might not be able to. As much as the responsibility mainly lies on parents to bear the brunt of the weight when it comes to helping their children, there is also nothing wrong with relying on grand parents, the people around you to help out and play their role too.

10. Express how you feel

As your teens are older and more mature, they are able to relate to the emotions you may be feeling more so than they would have as a child. Being open and vulnerable to your children is an important factor to getting them to open up themselves. Rather than bottling your own emotions up, show your children that everyone faces extreme experiences as well and this will give them the opportunity to see that everyone also goes through things and they will therefore not feel as alone. While this is a way to show your children the realities that adults are faced with, it does not mean putting added pressure and burdening them with the problems that you are faced with. This is another means for your child to relate to you and therefore feel encouraged to share their own life more openly and willingly with you.

11. Professional help

Consider speaking to a professional if you find that you are unable to really grasp what your teen might be going through, whether it is because of reluctance on your teen's part to share or if the issue is more serious than you are able to help him manage. There is no shame in seeking professional help because it gives your teen a neutral party to speak to who provides a safe, judgement-free space for them to express themselves. This does not mean you are any less of a parent, in fact, it makes you a commendable one for recognizing your own strengths and weaknesses and ultimately placing your child's health over your own ego. Many parents struggle with the blow that their ego faces for they believe that speaking to a professional means that they are not a good parent. This is definitely not the case. Many teens recognize their parents' limitations and appreciate the degree of seriousness they treat their mental health.

Join other parents Raising Children | Facebook

The severity of what your child may be going through can vary in degrees. Ultimately, it is up to you to take the right steps and help them express their feelings and manage their emotions appropriately in a way that is sustainable and relieving. Mental health is crucial for a teen during this age, so take it incredibly seriously and be proactive in helping your teen.

Your free gift!

AS A WAY OF SAYING THANK YOU
FOR
PURCHASING THIS BOOK, I AM
OFFERING YOU A FREE GIFT AT THE
END OF THE BOOK

*P*lacing limitations on your teen boys on what they can or cannot do can be incredibly discouraging. Helping them find their passions can be one of the more exciting parts of parenting because as you are exposing your child to the possibilities of the world, they are learning a great deal about themselves and finding themselves. Hobbies are one of the best ways to do this. Traditionally, parents would limit their children in sports because of the idea of masculinity. However, as we have progressed as a society and continue to disregard these gendered ideas, it opens teen boys up to an endless world of new things to try to develop their creative and logical sides that can stay with them well-into their adulthood and for the rest of their lives. Fostering creativity for teen boys can often stump parents because they are still thinking in the framework of gender, where certain activities are exclusive to girls only. But when we rid this idea all together, we can see that there are plenty of options to foster creativity.

Some parents might question the need to foster creativity. Ultimately, it lies in the fact that as humans, we have some inclination towards creativity, expression and the arts. There are plenty of benefits to encourage your children to be creative and there are plenty. With TV and computer screens more commonly becoming the object of your kids' obsession during their teen years, fostering creativity is a great way to primarily, get them away from their reliance on video games and watching TV all day. Creative development is a great way to teach your children how to think outside of the box and problem solve. Teens are able to develop their reasoning and logic as well as formulate their own ideas independently without interference from teachers or their parents. Creativity opens up a whole world of possibilities for your children to explore in terms of art, dance, music, and many more. As children age, what can sometimes happen is that creativity is placed on the back burner as they face more intense curriculums in school. However, the need for creativity will most certainly come up during their adult life. Fostering divergent thinking from a young age will help them when they enter the workplace or higher education as they will be met with a multitude of challenges and hardship that will require thinking outside of the box. This is why it is crucial for parents to continue encouraging creative thinking and recognize the value of the benefits that arise out of this early on in your parenting journey and in your child's development.

Particularly for boys, creative development is often placed on the back burner because of the fact that physical education or mathematics and logic are instead deemed more acceptable for this gender. But as it has been reiterated, it lies within parents to recognize how this can really impede on your children's development. Placing them in boxes and labelling them and thus creating even more limitations only hinders them in the long run. So rather than raising boys to be masculine and encourage only "manly hobbies", choose to instead nurture their interests above all else.

A note about toxic masculinity: this is a social expectation that has been imposed on boys for centuries. This essentially forces men into thinking that in order to be masculine, they must hide their emotions, be dominant and have a strong physique. This imagery is extremely dangerous for young and impressionable teens as they are constantly being bombarded with this idea of the "ideal man" through social media like Instagram. This pressure is counterproductive and can have a profoundly negative impact on how men view their self-worth and in turn view women and others around them. Having a conversation about toxic masculinity with your teen is a good way to educate your child about creating attainable goals that are realistic and beneficial for not only themselves, but for society as a whole. Toxic masculinity is a reason why certain hobbies are frowned upon for males and certainly why creativity is placed on the backburner when it comes to educating them.

The following is a list of hobbies that are often overlooked for boys or deemed "too girly". These are great activities to encourage your child's development.

1. Theatre

Theatre is an incredible platform to get your children to develop their self-confidence and public speaking skills. Acting, or even musical theatre can help uncover some untapped potential your teen may have. Theatre is also a social environment that many children thrive in as they are exposed to a cohort who provide support and friendship. Exposing your teen boys to new ways of communicating and is an effective and safe space to serve as an emotional outlet. Theatre is a good way to foster cooperation and another facet of responsibilities that your child may not necessarily have at home. It is another way to be a part of a team that is often overlooked, for "teams" often entail being part of sports, but theatre is another way to encourage experimentation and going out of their comfort zone while still in a group setting.

2. Stand-up comedy

Teenagerhood is a great time to foster this hobby. Not only does it encourage writing skills and independent thinking, it also places your teen in front of an audience. It's a great outlet to practicing communicative skills and a place to expel emotions in a way that gives them the satisfaction and immediate gratification of an audience. It is also a place where criticism is given freely, so it helps your teens grow a thicker skin and understand implementing changes and tweaking their routines to be better than the last. By the time your children are teenagers, it helps them While this hobby can seem out of the box, a number of drama schools and schools in general may feature courses or programs that you can enroll your children in to teach them the fundamentals of comedy for them to expand on.

3. Vlogging

The internet provides an infinite resource for your teen to develop themselves. Many teens have found success on YouTube as vloggers. Simply by sharing their daily lives and their journeys, teens are able to communicate and develop an understanding for an audience. Teens can also find their own niche of what they may want to share and develop their ideas in video format. This can teach them a slew of other skills from video editing to business management should they become successful and their popularity grows. It also encourages responsibility as your teens will have an audience to respond to.

4. Pottery

Pottery enables your teen to get to use their cognitive and tactile skills in order to produce creations. Through pottery, they are able to engage in a process that can help them concentrate and focus. Pottery is a quiet activity that can allow your teen time to destress and relax while also spending their time productively.

5. Dancing

With so many dance styles that exist, there is bound to be one that your teen son will enjoy. Dancing is especially beneficial because it gives your child another vantage point to understanding culture and learn about traditions and customs. It opens them to the world and its diversities and leads to empathy and respect for the differences that exist around us. In addition to this, it gives your teenage sons the physical activity that they may not be getting on a regular basis as they practice every day.

6. Skating

Whether your teen son chooses to skate professionally, competitively or recreationally, this is another way to get him moving and getting physical activity. It allows them to focus and express themselves through their body and movement. It promotes blood circulation and flexibility, things that are often overlooked for teens who are glued to their computer monitors constantly. Rather than being a violent sport, it encourages strength in a graceful way. Don't be fooled by how professionals make skating seem so effortless; it requires plenty of strength and discipline.

7. Gardening

This hobby is a good way to get your teen boys outside and getting in touch with their environment and nature around them. Learning about produce and flowers broadens your child's knowledge and exposes them to the world that exists outside. Gardening also involves being a nurturer, which is often not as emphasized for boys in the school curriculum or simply in their daily lives. It affords your teen son the responsibility of caring for another living thing while also allowing them to express their creativity by exploring the world beyond the confines of the inside.

8. Cooking

Similar to gardening, cooking is another way to foster creativity as your teen son learns their way around the kitchen and develops an understand for fruits, vegetables, seasonings and how they may all come together to create a final product that they can be proud of. This way, it also teaches sons that the kitchen is not a space that is exclusive to women only. Cooking is also an important life skill to have that your child should be prepared with as they mature and move on to the next stages of their lives.

9. Meditation/ Scripture reading

Meditation is a fantastic hobby to facilitate mental health in a positive and accepting environment. It's a great way to relax from the chaos of everyday life and to take a moment to breathe and focus on yourself, rather than everything going on around you. It also encourages self-reflection, which is always a good way to encourage positive thinking.

> *David found a secret which he shared to*
> *help all young people in the book of*
> *Psalm 119:9-11*
> *How can young people keep their lives*
> *pure?*
> *By obeying your commands.*

[10] With all my heart I try to serve you;
keep me from disobeying your
commandments.
[11] I keep your law in my heart,
so that I will not sin against you.
I John 2:14 says the same "I have
written to you, young men,
because you are strong,
the word of God abides in you,
and you have overcome the evil one."
Keeping the word of God and
obeying the instructions makes young
people strong.

Singing

Teen boys are often overlooked when it comes to pursuing singing. There are plenty of singing styles that will appeal to your son and their preferences and pique their interest. Many boys sing prior to puberty but feel the need to stop once their voices have changed. This certainly does not have to be the case. Through singing, they are able to explore interests in music and develop a deeper understand for theory and another facet of culture.

These hobbies have been featured here especially because of the stigma that surrounds them for teen boys who fear pursuing these hobbies. Your own kids may feel resistant to wanting to pursue these hobbies, and this is a great opportunity to discuss why and talk about the inherent biases that exist in our minds. Take the opportunity to explain to your teen boys that there is nothing wrong with wanting to pursue these hobbies, especially if they already have an interest in them and want to continue them but are afraid of criticism. Being a source of support and reassurance for your teen boys helps them build confidence and encourages them to pursue their interests wholeheartedly and dedicatedly.

Additionally, certain skills are often overlooked when it comes to raising boys as parents stick to stereotypes and adhere to gender roles and the so-called duties of each gender. This ends up setting your son up for failure as they will be unprepared for survival in the real world. There are a number of skills that many men are unfamiliar with because they were coddled and taught that they were the job of women.

- Basic household chores: both sons and daughters must have an understanding of how to run a household. Assigning housework and chores is not limited to women only. Doing dishes, laundry and other basic chores teaches sons to have basic cleanliness and responsibility over their environment.

- Basic cooking: being able to cook is a means of survival. Parents tend to assume that sons are simply disinterested in cooking and again, this can be a huge generalization. Teaching them the very basics is a way to prepare them for when they move out and gives them the ability to be more self-sufficient.

- Understanding the female body: plenty of men are still unsure of how the female body works, especially with periods, PMS and even pregnancy. While you don't have to get down to the nitty gritty of details, having a basic understanding of biology will help your sons have a better understanding of the world in general. Plenty of males avoid this education because it is deemed to be not in their realm, but it is equally important to understand these things as it is to understand their own biological processes.

HANDLING ANGER AS A PARENT

*D*isciplining older children can be difficult for parents to face because it can be more complex than disciplining younger children. Because your children are older now, they expect an increased amount of independence and discipline from parents simply does not fall into that category. Many teens see their parents' discipline as a form of control or being overtly strict and not trusting them with the freedom that they think they might have deserved. So, when it comes down to it, your disciplining techniques might be met with reluctance and even rebellion. Teens will continuously test your patience and the limits of their independence while you attempt to strike the balance as they enter this new stage of adolescence.

As they experience new and extreme emotions from physical, emotional and social changes through puberty and aging, this time can be tumultuous for them. This is where you as the parent enter in order to help adolescents grapple with these big changes, and sometimes it might mean disciplining them and taking away their privileges in order for them to learn that there are consequences to their actions. Particularly during these formative years, serious mental health issues can emerge at this time. Most commonly, we see depression and anxiety manifesting as your teen goes to school and is faced with social interactions that can be negative. A deteriorating mental health can be attributed to a number of things and there never is one simple answer because it is so complex and difficult to come to terms with.

The techniques you use may take some getting used to as every teen is different and is growing up in varying environments. Ultimately, it lies on you to know your child and distinguish what will and will not be best for them, especially when it comes to imparting lessons. Adolescence is the time for parents to relinquish their reins on guiding their children and strike a good balance between giving them freedom while still guiding them through life. For many teens, this means less supervision, later curfews, or simply arguing with the decisions you may have made for them. Teens want to be able to do things in their own way and at their own time and being told what to do by authoritative figures like their parents or teachers is the antithesis to this. Teenager-hood also means breaking rules. Your teens may disagree with your decision to not allow them to go to a party and may sneak out or lie to get out of your rules.

From a parents' point of view, this time is especially difficult because it may seem like your child is doing everything in their power to test you and frustrate you. Teens are going to constantly push the envelope when it comes to rules and regulations and for you, the best way to cope with this is to remember that they will grow out of this phase. Stay calm and always remember to never act out of anger. As always, children are wired to mimic others and extreme responses like anger when you're frustrated can reflect in your children as well. That is not to say that you are not allowed to be angry. But managing your anger, frustration and stress in a healthy way is crucial for both you and your children.

The following are some tips for parents to healthily manage anger or frustration:

1. Breathe

Taking a few moments to pause and breath to process the situation. This is extremely important because it allows you to try and logically think things through; like how the situation may have escalated and how to bring it back to the point that is civil and respectful. But before you even begin to try and put pieces together in a situation that your child is involved in, take a second to just breathe in and out and count silently to ten. Getting into the right framework is important to thinking things through logically.

2. "This too shall pass"

Your children did not stay in their terrible twos forever. Likewise, this teenage rebellion will also eventually phase out, provided that you are supplying them with the right consequences and imparting them with lessons that they need to learn. In order to grow out of this phase and for this time of backtalking and disrespect to stop, you have to nip it in the bud early-on so that your teens can decipher right from wrong in terms of appropriate and acceptable behaviours and attitudes. Failure to do so will result in meltdowns in their adulthood that is most definitely inexcusable and out of question for acceptable adult behaviours.

3. Step away

Parents often send their children to their bedrooms for their children to reflect on their poor behaviour before having a talk with them. This strategy works because not only do kids get a chance at self-reflection, but so do adults. This is the time to think about what punishment your child will receive and the conversation that needs to be heard about curbing poor behaviour or attitudes.

4. Listen to your anger

Anger can often lead us to do things we might regret immediately. Rather than acting out of anger, approach your anger critically and try to think rationally. Sometimes your children may act in a way that is aggravating and frustrating that may warrant getting angry, especially if they endanger themselves or do things that you have explicitly told them not to do. However, in some cases, anger can form irrationally when your children do not deserve it. Rather than immediately acting on the anger that forms, consider why exactly you feel this way. For example, sometimes you might be taking your anger out on your kid after a long and stressful day at work. Your child is not your emotional punching bag, so always be wary of how you are responding to your emotions.

5. Avoid physical punishment

Spanking and slapping your children never teaches them anything constructive, aside from making them fear you. Hitting your children can have a profoundly negative impact on your child's development that can last throughout their lives. Being hurt by a parent completely destroys trust and a strong foundational basis. So while you may feel angry and frustrated, the answer is never to spank your children in your rage. It can render all of the positive things you have done as a parent completely useless because your child will grow to fear your punishment and find ways to work around it.

6. Assert authority

While your children should not fear you, they should definitely respect you as an authoritative figure in their lives. Reacting out of anger can often inspire threats that are unreasonable, which will in turn undermine your authority. Rather than immediately punishing them with threats that will not be followed through, take some time to think about an appropriate punishment that will make them learn and understand why they are being punished in the first place.

METHODS TO DISCIPLINE
TEEN BOYS

Once you have recognized that you are in a situation where your child will have to be disciplined, parents are often unsure of how to go about actually disciplining their teen boys. While these techniques are absolutely interchangeable and appropriate to be used on your teen girls as well, here are some strategies for you to employ:

1. Remove electronics

Screen time is important to most teenagers, with their cellphones, laptops and TVs being readily available to them. Cellphones in particular are crucial for a teen's social life, with social media being a source of entertainment and fun. Restricting these privileges can really get your message across to your teenager. By placing time limits, your teens will be compelled to reflect on their behaviour and encouraged to rethink their attitudes for the next time.

2. Restrict time with friends

Misbehaviour can manifest in many forms and sometimes your children may not be acting alone. You absolutely can take away their right to see their friends for a while. By restricting them for a few days or cancelling a plan they might have had as a consequence, this will serve as a reminder to make the better choices next time.

3. Tighten the rules

When your teen knowingly violates the rules that you have laid out, this may be a way for them to convey that they are unable to handle the new freedoms and independence that teenagerhood may bring. Giving them an earlier curfew might curb some of their inability to handle the newfound freedom that brings about recklessness and rebellion. Consider tightening the rules and changing them up in order to better suit your child's development.

4. Not all consequences will be imparted by you

Natural consequences can occur from certain situations and they can provide an even better learning lesson for your kids. But it's important to make sure the natural consequences will really teach your teen something important that they will hold onto. This is your chance to let your children be independent and allow them to face the natural consequences that occur from their actions. For example, teens quickly understand that forgoing their homework and studying will impede their chances for getting into a good college or university. Some choose to test this and push the envelope by neglecting these responsibilities. The natural consequence of this is that they will face a difficult time when it comes to applying to college because their grades are simply not up to par. As much as you want your children to succeed, sometimes they need to experience the consequences in order to take their responsibilities seriously.

5. Provide logical consequences

Create consequences that are directly tied to the poor decisions your teen chose to make. As they are older and feel more inclined to make their own decisions, creating consequences in this way also has the benefit of preparing them for what is to come as they enter into adulthood. For example, if your teen breaks something of value deliberately, make them pay to fix it. Or, if they are irresponsible with driving and the car, take away their driving privileges. These are logical and realistic consequences that will happen in the real world as well. They are not just limited to the household.

6. Assign extra responsibilities

Sometimes children need to earn back the privileges they may have gotten in the process of maturing. Take away their privileges and assign extra work for them to complete, like chores or helping out around the house in order for them to earn back the trust that they have broken.

7. Be consistent

Mean what you say when you decide to discipline your child. Decide on the best course of action and the important part is to stick with it, no matter how angry or upset your teen may be getting. Setting a pattern of consequences to your teen's poor behaviour and attitude will get through to them that all actions have immediate consequences that they will have to face.

8. Know your teen

Understand your teen's personality in order to figure out the healthiest and most effective consequences for your teens. Knowing what they are motivated by and the privileges that they treasure is a great place to start in order to determine the best course of action. This means that you must foster a strong relationship with them with open communication lines and judgement-free conversations. This is your chance to be more of a friend to your child as they divulge their personal details and share the things that may be bothering them or weighing down on them. Or on the flipside, they may tell you about the areas that they are thriving in. Mentally catalogue these things and keep up with the changes in their lives like friends that come and go as these facts will come in handy when trying to parent your children.

9. Walk away

If you find that your teen is being disrespectful towards you and saying things that are extremely hurtful or being overly argumentative, sometimes one of the best ways to curb this is to simply walk away. You may choose to say something like "Until you can speak to me like an adult, I won't be having this conversation with you." Then follow up with a privilege being taken away. This way, your child will have no one to argue with and will be forced to revaluate the way they are speaking to you in order to regain their consequences. This is also the time to talk to them about how they externalize their anger. Speaking rudely to a parent is never the way for them to get their point across.

Disciplining your children can be a stressful and complicated aspect of raising kids that many parents dread but the reality is that it is completely necessary in order to teach them the appropriate way of life. Employ these tactics to try and teach them why good behaviour and attitudes in response to the various situations that will arise in their lifetime. Teaching children to cope and manage from a young age is a valuable skill to have as it will follow them well-into adulthood. While these consequences might seem exclusive to the parent and child dynamic, many parallels can be drawn for when your children enter the real world.

*A*s much as punishments are important for their development, there are a slew of other aspects that are also important to focus on when it comes to raising happy and healthy teenagers.

Focus on the positives in order to foster an encouraging environment for your teens. For adolescents, they are really just trying to figure things out at their own pace and time. Parents and teachers encourage teens because they have experience in how the real world works and the world will not always bend to their will or their pace. As much as your child will make mistakes and test their boundaries, constantly being on their case and punishing them for every mistake they make sometimes might be a counterproductive approach. Instead, encourage and praise them by placing an emphasis on the positive actions and why they were positive.

Set clear expectations for your teens to follow. Having wild and elaborate schemes only set them up for failure. With so many authoritative figures and rules to remember, it is important that the rules you set are clear and concise so that your teens will see what is important to you. This is also a way to set them up to follow your rules if they are simple and fair. For example, expecting to be treated respectfully is a fair rule to have, and a basic expectation that every child must be accustomed to. Communicate your expectations effectively and talk to your children about your feelings and desires. Let him know what you expect from him and always be able to explain why so that they understand your logic as well. For example, let your teens know that A's and B's are acceptable grades for you because anything lower will hinder their route to college. Or make completion of homework a prerequisite before they hang out with their friends. Consider putting your expectations in writing, email or text it to him. This way, children will not be able to forget them as they will be a constant reminder.

Get your teenagers to open up to you by avoiding "yes" or "no" answers. Instead, talk to them about where they are thriving in school and where they may be struggling. Rather than berating them for doing poorly, this is a chance to come up with a plan together on how to move forward to be successful on their next test on exam. To develop a strong relationship with your teens as they spend an increasing amount of time away from home, constantly ask them how their education is going, who their new friends are. And how their extracurricular activities might be going. Setting time aside to talk to them about how things are going can really help your teens grapple with the complex emotions and relationships they might be experiencing.

Whatever your household expectations are about relationships, this is the time to show your support for your children by encouraging them to discuss their lives. Parents find this aspect of their teens growing up incredibly uncomfortable, but it is usually better for you to have assumptions about your teen, rather than not. This way you can prepare them for what is out there and warn them about the dangers that exist.

Validate your childrens' feelings by being an active listener. As much as communicating with them is important, listening is equally as important to be a good source of support for your kids. Offer them feedback and try to provide them with advice if they ask you for it. Validate how they are feeling and be specific when you acknowledge their feelings. It helps teens feel heard and understood because of this time period in their life being so volatile and complicated.

One of the biggest challenges parents face during this

time is learning when to let go of their children and give them the independence they need to thrive and find their place in the world. The teenage years are crucial for this very reason. Not relinquishing control over your children can lead to disastrous effects as adolescents and parents will become at odds with each other. Children will resent their parents for their overcontrolling nature, while parents will continue to face frustration and disappointment constantly because their child refuses to listen to them.

Finding that balance is the biggest tip that can be taken away from this book. Understanding where your child thrives and where they fall short is how to build the foundational blocks to help them develop mentally and socially. For parents, this is the biggest challenge because they seek to be a friend to their children while also being an authoritative figure that they respect.

When your children are young, you dictate every aspect of their lives; from what time they eat, what time they sleep, what they watch, etc. Teens are the exact opposite of this as they immediately feel able to handle the responsibilities that adulthood may bring and experience a surge of confidence that comes with transitioning from into the adolescent age group. This is the time where adolescents feel like they are able to control their destiny and make their own decisions.

Teenagerhood is a time for parents to recognize that this is where they need to allow their children to flourish independently. When kids reach adolescence, they need to prepare for adulthood by their own terms and parents have to foster this need to be independent so that they are able to flourish. Attempting to dictate their lives by your schedule every single day and controlling every part of their lives will eventually lead to them defying you the first chance they get and finding ways around your punishments and consequences.

This by no means entails that this is the parent's chance to relax and completely release their attention or time on their teens. While parents are not the immediate influence on their children anymore, they still play a huge role in their lives as a constant source of stability and comfort as they are involved in their child's life. By shifting our focus onto our teens and letting them dictate the course of their lives, this means that your children will get a chance to make mistakes and learn some real-life lessons that need to be taught and not necessarily by you. Your job here is to provide them with the guidance and emotional support that they need to get through the challenges life presents them.

Raising teenagers is not an easy thing because your kids will argue and have a differing view from you. Parents often feel helpless when they have especially argumentative kids as they feel like they're simply not getting through to them. But ultimately, it is how you deal with these difficult times with your children that have the greatest impact on them and will stay with them for the rest of their lives, so never rush when it comes to disciplining your children. Your influence now has to evolve along with your kids. Because they have this inherent need to be indepedent, simply telling them what to do can lead to even more arguments and strife between the parent and child dynamic. Some parents take this time to instead treat their children like an adult to respect their choices and find the balance that is needed where you are still an authoritative figure that they seek guidance from. Talk to them like you would with other adults and do not sugar-coat things. Teens want to be able to know they are in control of the situation, rather than feel lesser than and unable to make decisions for themselves.

As soon as puberty hits, a string of uncertainties and new developments will arise that your children might not respond well to. They may attempt to deal with changes personally and privately, but sometimes they may yearn support from their parents in order to navigate through whatever they may be going through, whether it is mentally, physically or socially. In order to really provide the support that your child needs, you will have to discuss uncomfortable topics with them.

This can be an extremely daunting task but it is incredibly crucial to provide support for your teens, especially if they are boys because boys are more often than not encouraged to keep their personal feeling and emotions bottled up in comparison to their female counterparts.

Featured below is a condensed list of important subjects to broach with your children, regardless of their gender.

- Mental health: Prioritize your child's mental health just as you prioritize their physical health. Boys are often told to bottle up their feelings and in order to curb this, start by having discussions about their feelings and what they may be experiencing. This is a way to show them that their feelings are valued and allowed. It also shows them that you care for their mental wellbeing.
- Sexual activity: Teen years means engaging in relationships which can lead to sexual activity. While schools provide health education, make sure to reiterate to your teens with the talk. Be open and blunt with your teens about the dangers and temptations (You can get more in chapter 6 of my book."The Child Development and Positive Parenting Master Class :Proven Methods for Raising Well-Behaved and

Intelligent Children, with Accelerated Learning Methods " My Book

- Alcohol and drugs: Be open and blunt with your teens about the dangers and temptations of alcohol and drugs. You want to be able to trust them to make the right decisions if they are ever faced with substances, especially when they are underage. Educating them on the dangers that these substances pose is incredibly crucial to making sure that they are well-informed when they are faced with tough situations.

- Internet safety: Social media and the internet are a huge part of most teenagers' lives. It plays a massive impact on molding adolescence and teens can often get so caught up on the latest internet trends. Impart on them safe procedures online, like withholding personal information and protecting their identity. Furthermore, it is important to reiterate that social media is extremely superficial. Social media can have a negative impact on your child's self-esteem and confidence, so having a healthy relationship with Instagram, Facebook and Twitter are important to develop.

- Saying 'no': The word no is not reiterated enough for teens. Educate your children on potential uncomfortable and dangerous threats that exist out in the world and provide them with a way out by letting them know that should they ever be in an uncomfortable situation, you will always be there to support them and help them.

PLEASE LEAVE A 1-CLICK REVIEW!

I hope you enjoyed reading this book!

If you haven't done so yet, I would be incredibly thankful if you could take 60 seconds to write a brief review on Amazon or the platform of purchase , even if it's just a few sentences!

Your feedback will be a huge help in helping other readers benefit from the information in the book.

You can also contact us by sending an email to tcecpublishing@outlook.com

Like us on https://www.facebook.com/tcecpublishing/

Join our Facebookpagehttps://www.facebook.com/groups/397683731371863/ to stay updated on our next releases!

See you there!

CONCLUSION

Raising sons and daughters can be equally as challenging and fighting the gender roles that are assigned to them can be extremely difficult as your child enters the education system and faces various influences in their lives that will constantly reiterate these labels. However, establishing that your sons are able to flourish and respect their way of life is the first step to breaking down some of the societal expectations that are simply unrealistic and illogical. The fact that cooking has historically been deemed a "woman's job" is simply unrealistic in the twenty-first century and beyond. In order to raise self-sufficient and responsible sons, rid yourself of the inherent biases you may have and focus on wholeheartedly bringing up your teen sons to succeed in their lives in whatever way they choose to do so. Instead of encouraging them to follow the status quo, provide them with the tools they need to nurture their personal likes and dislikes.

Teen boys are faced with their own set of identity related issues as they grapple with the framework of masculinity that is imposed on them. Some boys choose to act within this framework, while plenty choose to break gender stereotypes and define their own way. Regardless of what they may choose, it is a parents' duty to encourage and support their decisions and be their cheerleader. Help them nurture their natural instincts, follow the leading of their conscience and preferences.

Young people have so much untapped potential that society will end up stifling because of the strict norms that are continuously enforced through its institutions like schools and workforce. These highly gendered environments place an emphasis on traditional male and female stereotypes which greatly limit teens altogether. It can have a profound impact on a person's well-being and really hinder confidence. However, this can all be controlled and completely disregarded in the household, where parents are able to control the message that they want to send out to their children. Rather than focusing on these traditional stereotypes, choosing to instead foster true-love and confidence in your own abilities is a good way to teach your children that it is perfectly acceptable to be themselves, no matter what society may tell them.

Toxic masculinity can subconsciously worm its way into your teen's consciousness through social media or even their peers and the interactions that they have. Establishing early on that this is a harmful way of thinking can save your teenage son a lot of grief and hardship as they grapple with their identity in the process of maturing and aging. Establish that they are not defined by society's harmful standards of masculinity and encourage them to develop their own identity that they are comfortable with and proud of from their maker's perspective which is known more when they read the scriptures..

The challenge comes in at the key part of successfully raising sons (and children in general), which is to strike a balance between allowing them to express themselves freely and disciplining them should they cross the line. It is an incredibly difficult task that many parents find daunting and at times, impossible to do. But now, armed with the tips and techniques of this books, you will be able to find that balance in your household in order to raise sons that follow the appropriate conventions of life while also flourishing in their own space.

While this book discusses disciplining teens and how parents can be extremely frustrated or angered by behaviours, it is also crucial to note how parenting itself is an incredible privilege and a joy as you watch your children grow and develop. Parents are able to see the knowledges that they imparted on their kids from a young age come out when they are older and the pride that is associated with your child growing up to be good people is indescribable. Disciplining your children can seem like a dreaded thing but it is simply one of the many facets that is part of being a parent. There are always going to be upsides and downsides to everything.

PARENTING TEEN GIRLS IN TODAY'S CHALLENGING WORLD

PROVEN METHODS FOR IMPROVING TEENAGERS BEHAVIOUR WITH WHOLE BRAIN TRAINING

INTRODUCTION

While it is difficult to say if one gender is inherently harder to raise than the other, being a girl and more specifically, a teenage girl can be an incredibly complicated and difficult time as the female body experiences extreme changes that can certainly scare and even traumatize young girls. There are a number of biological differences that can affect both men and women and for women, hormonal changes can greatly impact a female's mental health and wellbeing. Additionally, societal expectations on the role of females limit them as they age. Females are subjected to glass ceilings and a number of biases that males will never understand.

For parents raising teenage girls, this can be a breeze for many as girls tend to be more resourceful and independent at this age compared to their male counterparts. However, that isn't to say that all girls are this way, and it certainly depends on the environment they are raised in and the childhood influences that play a huge part in shaping teens and their later years. Parents are faced with the normal teenage woes and have to deal with the set of problems that come with being a teenage boy or a teenage girl. In general, for teenage girls, the social norm that has been established allows them ask for help or receive help and affection. Facing emotional issues tends to be a more common problem seen in teenage boys.

So, when it comes to raising boys and girls, techniques catered to specific genders simply do not exist because the issues that each gender deals with can be so diverse and unique to each individual. Rather than seeing teen girls and boys are groups and making huge, sweeping generalizations about how they may act, a more a effective way is to see your child as an individual and treat them as such. This way, you are able to get a better understanding of the issues they may be facing and cater to their needs.

Seasoned parents would argue that teenagerhood is the most difficult time for parenting. Many parents might say that this time period for your teenagers is a time of high emotions and added pressure as your teenager experience leaving their childhood and are on the cusp of adulthood. Your teens are in the process of making big decisions that will affect their futures, particularly with their educations and careers which is an incredibly stressful time for most. Teens could be experiencing more complex relationships and the emotions associated with that. Additionally, as your children age, they become more accustomed to the fact that the world is more flawed than what they might have been used to during their protected childhood years that featured a far more idealistic and positive view. As your children age, they are met with the responsibilities that they will have to take on as adults. With all of these in mind, the immense stress that can weigh on a teen's mental health during this time can be immense. With this transition of age being so formative and crucial for your teens, the same stress and pressure reflects onto parents as well, which is why teenagerhood is seen as a particularly difficult time for both parents and children alike.

However, that is not to say that techniques don't exist for raising respectable and good-hearted teens. It comes down onto parents instilling these good values into their teens so that they can carry these life lessons with them well into adulthood and practice them. As much as gender stereotyping should be discouraged, there are a few inherent differences between boys and girls that should be differentiated and discussed when raising girls and boys. However, keep in mind that all of the tips that are introduced in these books are interchangeable between genders and can be applied to any teen as they have no prerequisites or preconditions that need to be followed before being applied. These tips are universally applicable and really serve to nurture your teen's interests and needs, regardless of their gender.

These books are here to provide a framework for raising your teens. They are great resources to understand what your child may be going through during this especially volatile time. Refer to this books companion piece if you are raising a son and seek to understand the challenges that they may be facing.

*R*aising teenage daughters does not necessarily have to be a difficult thing. What becomes difficult is establishing the balance between the parent and child dynamic because of the inherent need to be an authoritative figure while also maintaining a close connection with their daughter. Striking this balance is important but also one of the biggest challenges that parents are faced with when raising their teenage daughters because of the extreme changes that they are going through. While parents have to discover the best way to parent their kids, they also have to evolve alongside them and accept that times are changing where their children seek to be more independent by their own terms during this stage of their lives. While their bodies are changing, so are their minds. Parents have to deal with the fact that their children simply do not require them as much as they did when they were younger and more reliant on them for their survival. This is the time for them to start dipping their toes in the water and finding their way through the challenges of life. It is incredibly important for your kids to learn things by themselves and avoid feeding them the answers to everything.

While your teenage daughter is growing, the emotional impact that puberty has on a girl should not be underestimated. You will see changes manifest in a number of different ways, or perhaps even a combination of all of the following. Girls tend to be greatly underestimated and their emotions tend to be brushed off because of the stereotypes that exist that encourage a mindset that females are too emotional. Not only is this a dangerous mindset, but it also completely sweeps all of the issues your daughter may be going through under the rug. It is incredibly important to be perceptive of the changes they may be going through because they may not be immediately comfortable with sharing these private details with you. It is equally important to listen to them and validate their feelings and act on them if they need help. Some parents may struggle with trying to identify if their daughter may be going through a hard time. Here are some signs to look out for if you suspect your teenage daughter is experiencing difficulty.

1. Changing tides

Physical developments and changes that puberty brings can trigger body and self-esteem issues for your teenage daughter. It is not uncommon for self-consciousness to manifest during this time period as teens experience the discomfort of acne and other changes to their appearance. This can trigger a lifetime of harmful or self-destructive behaviour if not taken seriously from the get-go.

2. Mood swings

While TV shows and movies depict an often exaggerated and cliched version of how teenage daughters face mood swings, there is some truth to the stereotype as teen girls tend to show more varying degrees of sadness and happiness levels throughout their daily lives as societal expectations allow girls to be more expressive of their emotions and feelings, while males do not experience this in the same way.

3. Independence

Puberty does not just entail biological changes. As teenagerhood is a time to express independence, this can manifest in many different ways. Some girls may choose to dress differently and express themselves through their fashion. Some may choose to try out different hobbies or activities. The possibilities here are endless.

4. Body image

Body image impacts teen girls especially more profoundly and girls tend to focus on their outward appearances because of how drastic the changes can be. Additionally, the constant presence and availability of social media and edited pictures that circulate the internet and have become common place create unrealistic expectations of beauty for young girls to aspire towards.

5. Friendships

Friend groups, particularly among girls, can sometimes be especially volatile. There is some truth in the stereotype of girls flocking in cliques. Your daughter may be on the receiving end of the negative aspect of this and might be experiencing loneliness or even alienation from their social circles. Knowing how your child is doing socially is especially crucial during these formative years because it can greatly leave a lasting negative impact if left unattended.

6. Relationships

At this age, teenagers may be acting on romantic impulses and experiencing their first loves and consequently, their first heartbreaks. I have seen these many times in the schools and this can be an extremely vulnerable time that may result in them going through difficult emotions as they grapple with new relationships and the pressures associated with a relationship. Good counselling and guide has helped in school and could help at home as well.

7. Bullying

Bullying can manifest in many forms during a teen's life. It can have a profound impact on your teen's personality and behaviour that can follow them well-into adulthood if not dealt with appropriately early on.

8. Peer Pressure

During this time, teens want to feel like they belong and are part of a group and identify with the people around them. But peer pressure can introduce its own pressures and put your teens into uncomfortable situations that they might not be sure how to get out of.

9. Substance Use

Drugs and alcohol make themselves more known during this time period of your teen's life. Peer pressure can play a huge impact in this as your teen might find themselves back into a corner where they feel like they have to try these dangerous substances. Or they may rely on alcohol or drugs to relieve the stress they may be experiencing.

10. Mental health

Whatever the cause may be, your teen's mental health will be impacted in some way during their most formative years. It can manifest in a number of negative ways, from social anxiety to depression. There are plenty of things that can affect a teen's mental health; from friends and social interactions, break up, parental pressures, academic pressures...the list goes on.

Your free gift!

AS A WAY OF SAYING THANK YOU
FOR
PURCHASING THIS BOOK, I AM
OFFERING YOU A FREE GIFT AT THE
END OF THE BOOK

FREE

*O*nce you have identified where your teen daughter might be struggling, developing a plan of action to help them cope with their problems can be extremely daunting and stressful as you ultimately want the best for your child. But it is incredibly necessary if you want to impart healthy and appropriate coping mechanisms into your daughter from a young age.

1. Self-image

The issues that arise out of self-image issues can be diverse and extreme. It can manifest in the form of eating disorders and body dysmorphia. While boys can also go through the same thing, girls experience an added pressure on their outward appearance during their teenage years. To cope with this, monitor your teen closely, especially at the dinner table. Notice their eating habits and make sure that they are getting plenty of fruits and vegetables. Have an open line of communication to discuss how Photoshop can greatly alter how females look and that a person's worth is not based on how they look. Instill in them that being healthy is ultimately the most important thing. Teach your daughter the importance of self-worth by encouraging her to have positive role models in her life.

2. Relationship

This can be an especially complex thing to relate to your children with because young love can be innocent yet also complex in its own way. Especially from an adult's perspective, trying to relate to your teenage daughter's experiences can be doubly challenging but this is the time to educate your teenage daughter on sex. Sex Education should by no means be a taboo subject because you want to be able to impart on her the importance of keeping herself. While schools have health subjects, it is important to teach her biological processes and give her a basic understanding of how pregnancy can happen. Be open and honest and share with them without sugar-coating things and do not treat this subject as taboo because it will be a sign to her to bottle up her feelings and feel ashamed. The absolute last thing you want for your daughter is to be ashamed and have a life long regret for making her own independent decisions.

3. Bullying

This can be an extremely difficult subject for your daughter to broach because of a myriad of reasons. They may feel ashamed or scared of the consequences. They may think that bullying is their fault and may not understand that they do not deserve to be bullied. Make sure that you have a strong foundation with your daughter where you are able to recognize if she is shutting down or being more closed-off. This can be an indication that she is being bullied. Broaching the subject with her can be difficult and she may not feel comfortable sharing the details but reassuring her that you will support her and try your best to help her out of this tough situation can greatly ease the stress. Give her advice on how to face bullying and stand up for herself. If the issue is more severe, it may be time to step in and have a serious talk with her school.

4. Education

Teenagerhood can be a doubly stressful time for your kids' education because they are inching closer and closer to college and university. This added pressure can greatly affect your child's performance and more often than not, children can feel like their self-worth is tied to the grades they get. To tackle this, reassuring your child that you value hard-work and effort more so than grades. Low grades are not an indicator of any person's self-worth and consider finding an outlet for your child to engage in to destress and relax after school.

5. The power of "no"

It is also crucial to educate your daughter, above all else, the power of the word "no". Saying "no" can help your daughter out of situations and can even save her life. Your daughter has every right to say "no", especially when she is uncomfortable and while all parents would agree with this, many do not enforce this enough with their daughters. Prioritize teaching them this in their development. Your teens may need to practice this a few times with their family members in order to get comfortable with the idea of asserting their feelings but doing so is a good way to get accustomed to politely but firmly refusing someone.

6. Substance Use

Educate your kids about the detrimental side effects of drugs and alcohol, in addition to the consequences they face from illegal consumption as they are underage. Some teens in a discussion in the class argued and think the best way to combat this is to allow them to experience it in a controlled environment, like under their parents supervision. (The first trial is the only trial needed to be addicted)

hese techniques can be interchangeable with parenting teen boys as parenting in general requires being compassionate and empathetic to your child's struggles. These tips are a great place to start if you are unsure of how exactly to go about transitioning from raising a young girl to an adolescent. Ultimately, there is no "one size fits all" approach for raising a son or daughter and it may take some trial and error to find the perfect fit of balancing discipline and being their friend. Here are some tips for dealing with the challenges that raising a teenager can bring:

1. Communication is key

A lot of grief can be saved if your children simply communicate what they may be going through. But this just is not the case because of the complexities of emotions your teens are faced with. They may feel scared or intimidated and fear punishment or shame if they were to share their true feelings. Which means that it falls onto the parent to connect with their teens as much as they can and be an avid listener. Establish yourself as a trusted confidant and a safe space for them to share their deepest and darkest concerns.

2. Establish rules

Having realistic and logical boundaries that are concise and age-appropriate is crucial during this stage because teens want to challenge everything around them as they experience independence for the first time in their lives. Always expect that your rules will be broken, so be prepared with age-appropriate consequences that will teach your teens a lesson in a sustainable and effective way.

3. Don't take bad attitudes and behaviour personally

As much as your teen's words can hurt and cut deep, try your best to not take it personally. This does not mean that they will not receive consequences for being disrespectful but be prepared to be argued with and have your buttons constantly pushed as your teens test the boundaries and fight against any form of authority or control.

4. Healthy risks

While children at this age are attracted to pushing the boundaries and thus taking risks, this can be performed in a healthy way. Through travelling, physical challenges and new social situations, there are a plenty of ways to take healthy risks without endangering themselves or their health. Furthermore, parents have a better understanding of what their children might be up to when they engage in these activities, which greatly eases the mind. Encouraging these activities also broadens your child's horizons and diversifies their experiences and exposes them to a number of new and healthy ways of coping.

5. Compromise

As much as you have a developed a relationship with your teens and try your best to develop a parenting style that fits them best, sometimes you might have to compromise with your teen's whims that may seem outlandish. Sometimes you may have to accept that this is another way for them to express themselves during this time. While you cannot control every single outcome, finding a happy medium and compromising with your teen is a way to try and maintain some semblance of calm and happiness.

6. Express love and affection

Unconditional love is exactly that. Your children will constantly make mistakes and push the boundaries and you will as well as you try to help them navigate through their lives and face the challenges that will be presented. No one has the perfect answer or response to everything. What is crucial is that you take these mistakes and turn them into learning lessons for your kids to set an example of how to appropriately respond to situations of extreme emotions. Likewise, the backbone of everything you do when raising children is to practice unconditional love. This should not be leveraged or withheld because your child is exhibiting frustrating or difficult behaviours.

7. Express how you feel

As your teens are older and more mature, they are able to relate to the emotions you may be feeling more so than they would have as a child. Being open and vulnerable to your children is can greatly encourage them to do the same when you are trying to understand what they are going through. By sharing your own struggles, your children are able to see that adults too, make mistakes and are susceptible to challenges. Being open with your kids encourages them to want to share more because you are setting a clear example for how to share their feelings and avoid bottling them up. This can eventually implode and lead to unhealthy ways of coping and mental health issues like depression and anxiety.

8. Be compassionate

Your teen is experiencing struggles that to you may seem minute, but for them can be astronomical. Be compassionate to their struggles and try not to judge them too harshly as young age tends to be a slew of bad decision making and reckless behaviour. Instead, provide them the support they need; whether it's a shoulder to cry on or someone to keep them company while they go through the consequences that they are facing.

9. You won't always be right

Accept when you are wrong. Parents often struggle with this because they are so accustomed to telling their kids specifically what to do and they may be met with resistance as they age and enter adolescence. Take time to evaluate the situation and sometimes, you may be wrong too. It is far more effective and commendable to admit when you are wrong, as painful as it may be when you are in the face of an argument with your child, but it is the right thing to do.

10. Trust their judgement

As difficult as it may be relinquishing your hold on your kids, it is a natural consequence of your children growing up. When this happens, give them freedom to act on their own choices and trust that they are making the most informed call. Parents often want to step in and tell their kids exactly what to do but should they make a mistake, it turns into a learning lesson for them to take with them for the next time and the rest of your life.

11. Choose your battles

It is true that raising teens bring a lot of butting heads and arguments. Sometimes you have to simply let it be. Picking a fight every single time is not only frustrating for both parent and child, it can also encourage teens to want to rebel even more as your rules get stricter and increasingly tight. Pick your battles wisely and save yourself another day of arguments and fighting. Sometimes allowing your teens to decide things for themselves as long as they are not harming themselves or those around them is a way of compromising with the fact that they are growing up mand making their own choices.

12. Focus on positivity

Positive encouragement is a tried and true method to get your kids to feel more confident in themselves. Especially when your child is going through a hard time, this can be a reminder than not all moments will be tough and emotionally draining. Spending time with family and friends or pursuing their hobbies can give them a break from stressors and temporarily give teens a chance to focus on something else, rather than constantly obsessing over the issue at hand. If it's an appropriate time, try to encourage your teen to get away from the chaos and focus on something that they love to do to take their mind off of things briefly and help them clear their heads. While this is not a way to completely solve problems, it relieves stress which can have a huge impact on overall mental health.

13. Recognize their rights

Too often, parents view their children as young and impressionable which causes them to coddle their kids, even as they are in their teenage years. This not only stunts their development but can foster resentment as children do not feel seen or heard as an individual because they are constantly being treated as a child and not being given the freedoms that they feel like they deserve. Recognize that your children are growing up and that they deserve freedoms in this process. They are no longer babies whose every move has to be tended to and watched. Allowing your kids to explore the world on their own enables them to grow and flourish in their own way.

14. Respect goes both ways

While you expect your teens to respect you as an authority figure, respect their choices as well. Particularly during their teen years, your child may experiment and dabble in a new identity whether that is through fashion or their interests. It can manifest in a number of ways. Frustration can build when parents choose not to validate this new identity. While it may be a phase, it can also potentially not be. Treat your kids with the same respect that you expect for yourself. Respect their choices and understand that you may not like everything they do and they will not always turn to you for advice. Despite this, you should not hold a grudge or treat them any lesser than they are.

15. Professional help

Consider speaking to a professional if you find that you are unable to really grasp what your teen might be going through, whether it is because of reluctance on your teen's part to share or if the issue is more serious than you are able to help him manage. There is no shame in seeking professional help because it gives your teen a neutral party to speak to who provides a safe, judgement-free space for them to express themselves. This does not mean you are any less of a parent, in fact, it makes you a commendable one for recognizing your own strengths and weaknesses and ultimately placing your child's health over your own ego. Many parents struggle with the blow that their ego faces for they believe that speaking to a professional means that they are not a good parent. This is definitely not the case. Many teens recognize their parents' limitations and appreciate the degree of seriousness in which they treat their mental health.

BREAKING THROUGH THE PERPETUAL GLASS CEILING

*T*een girls are faced with a countless number of limitations within a patriarchal society that tells them what they can or cannot do. This is the reality of what females face in the real world and these can eventually develop into full psychological roadblocks that your children will have to face in their adulthood. As their parent, it is your responsibility to forewarn your daughters of the realities and vulnerabilities that girls have to face when outside of the household. These differences between genders are further fostered when your child enters the education system, particularly seen through the many education systems choose to segregate boys and girls during physical education classes. While education systems differ all around the world, the school system is often where these notions of gender and the applicable stereotypes are established within your child. By the time your child has entered their teen years, ideas of "running like a girl" or "acting like a boy" have firmly wormed their way into their mindset. It is an inevitable result of the education system.

The glass ceiling is an invisible barrier that prevents women from reaching the same potential as their male counterparts and women often feel the impact of this early on, particularly in their teen years as they are establishing their education and career. Your daughter will immediately notice male domination the minute she enters into the real world.

You may notice overlap of the following tips from the companion book entitled *Parenting Teen Boys in Today's Challenging World*. These tips are applicable regardless of your child's gender and should be seen as cardinal rules to successfully raising children. These are especially appliable in the case of breaking the glass ceiling for girls because it establishes stability and good role models for them to model after.

Here are some ways to set your daughter up to break her way through face some challenges head on.

1. Build self-confidence from an early age

Develop a strong sense of self from an early age within the household. With the teen years being so divisive and stress filled, being sure of oneself can greatly reduce the impact that these problems can bring. Rather than raising your child as a people pleaser, teach her to stand up for what she believes in and encourage her to use her voice. The realities of society will soon shut her down and often speak over her, so relying on her self-esteem and confidence and take her far as it will require her to use her voice unabashedly. Developing this early on can make this into an inherent part of who she is once she enters teenagerhood.

2. Direct your praise to her achievements, rather than appearance

Females tend to have an obsession with their view because we are constantly surrounded by it in society. Rather than focusing on how she looks, focus on her achievements and how she is doing academically, morally and character wise. This does not mean that you should never compliment your daughter on her appearance, but it does mean to be cognizant of the unintentional focus that people tend to have when it comes to women. Establish early one that your daughter is so much more than how she looks and her self-worth is not tied to her appearance or how conventionally beautiful she is. Establish that beauty comes in many forms. Inner beauty is most crucial as it is gold. 1 Peter 3 [3] Whose adorning let it not be that outward adorning of plaiting the hair, and of wearing of gold, or of putting on of apparel; [4] But let it be the hidden man of the heart, in that which is not corruptible, even the ornament of a meek and quiet spirit, which is in the sight of God of great price.

3. Be affectionate

Demonstrating warmth and affection to all your children equally, regardless of gender, allows them to feel a sense of security and comfort whenever they are in your presence. This ties in with giving them the courage to share with you what they may be going through as affection tells them that regardless of the mistakes that they have made, their parents will still love them.

4. Avoid the "boys will be boys" mentality

This dangerous mentality is often used as an excuse to brush off certain behaviours or attitudes seen in boys. Teaching your daughters that men have to be held equally as accountable for their actions allows them to see that there are consequences for inappropriate behaviours. This also ties in with a girl's self-worth, as valuing yourself means protecting yourself from people who might want to take advantage of you. In this regard, teaching girls that there is never an excuse for inappropriate behaviour encourages them to speak out and put an end to people getting away with unacceptable behaviours.

5. Be present

While parents are expected to loosen the reins, it by no means entails completely abandoning parenting all together. You represent a guide for your child to follow and model after, even into their adult lives. Being present in their lives means continuing the relationship and bond you share, even if you may feel like they simply do not need you anymore. Particularly when your daughter is attempting to break through the glass ceiling, having the unconditional and constant support of their parents reiterates that they are doing the right thing and will always have some form of stability even if their attempts at equality fail.

6. Be a guide

Your children look to you as their role model from the minute they are brought into this world. Especially for mothers, daughters look to you to see how you fight the everyday biases that are imposed onto you. Model for them how you would want them to act when faced in the same situation, regardless of how young they may be. Children are inclined to mimic their parents and recreate their behaviours because it is the best point of reference that they have. This way, for your teen daughter, you are providing her with solutions to everyday problems that she will inevitably face. Always be extremely conscious of the fact that your children are constantly watching you and by the time they are teens, they will use you own behaviour as an argument should you yourself stray away from the behaviour or attitude you are trying to impart on them.

7. Claiming worth

Form an early age, teach your daughters to evaluate their own beauty and competence by their makers terms. By encouraging this, your daughters will try to avoid tying their self-worth to frivolous things and by terms that have been set by other people. Instead, they follow the laid down standard from their makers perspective and create their own standards to live by and are able to determine what they deserve, despite the noise that will constantly bring them down and tell them they are lesser than.

8. Embrace a growth mindset

Because teens are so susceptible to mistakes, encouraging a "growth mindset" rather than a "fixed" one teaches your kids to learn from their mistakes and treat them as a learning lesson to develop themselves. This way, rather than focusing on the fact that they were wrong, focus on why exactly they did what they did. Should they be faced with the same situation, they will have a better understanding of how to appropriately respond. Ultimately, we are all human and while finding our purpose in life is complex but can be made easier by studying, meditating and obeying the scriptures, we are creatures that learn and have the capability to expand, diversify and grow; mentally and socially.

9. Make room for failure

Failure can be extremely disappointing at this young age because teens tend to fixate on being an outlier as they want to fit in and be part of a group. Rather than glossing over the fact that they have failed something or avoiding a discussion about it, teach them to approach it head-on in order to face their fears and frights and get used to confronting these uncomfortable and less than ideal aspects of life. Getting used to failing sets them up for a life of unexpected failures and having a healthy way of coping with them from an early age will help them greatly in the long run.

10. Focus on extending compassion

Encourage your children to treat themselves with kindness and acceptance. Self-loathing and hatred can manifest during these early ages of teenagerhood because your kids simply don't know how to cope with the pressures of everyday life, their academic performance and their changing bodies. These are immense stressors that weigh your teens down heavily. Rather than focusing on what they may be achieving all the time, focus on the language they use on themselves. Teach your teens to focus on their well-being by extending the kindness they would treat others with upon themselves. Understanding that every person is flawed and that we will never be able to please every single person we meet is something that we have to grapple with and get used to from a young age.

11. Avoid comparisons

Parents sometimes feel inclined to compare our own kids to how our neighbour's kids might be doing. Everyone is at different aspects of their journeys and we have to respect that our children will go through their own unique journey. Rather than comparing them to others, compare your kids with where they were last year. Encourage them by pointing out how much they have developed in character and matured. Focus on spiritual, educational and self-development in a healthy and sustainable way.

12. Social media

Platforms like Instagram can have a negative impact on the way your teen views herself and her self-worth. It also places a huge emphasis on appearance. Social media and the concept of "likes" can seriously affect your child's development and foster jealousy and envy which can further lead to depression and anxiety. Encourage them to take breaks away from social media by nurturing their hobbies and interests.

Adolescence is a time that is filled with self-doubt and for many teen girls, this may be a time of struggle as they view themselves with a new light of insecurities. Establishing with your kids early on that their self-worth is not directly tied with their outward appearance is an important lesson that needs to be learnt. In order for your daughters to feel confident in their convictions, employ these strategies that encourage self-growth and improvement and focuses on efforts rather than imme- diate outcomes. Teaching your daughters to be assertive and having the ability to speak up for themselves in an appropriate way will help re-establish a sense of confi- dence within themselves. A teen who can speak up for themselves is also less likely to be bullied or bullied for very long because their self-worth is perceived in a different and positive light. As it has been reiterated, the best way for your kids to understand and grasp this behaviour and attitude quickly is if parents themselves model this behaviour so that their kids can have a first-hand view of how confidence and self-assuredness can greatly benefit them. Facing situations with courage really helps your teen in the long run.

What is possibly the most difficult aspect of encouraging positive thinking is to instill in your teens to thinking positively about themselves. A person's inner monologue plays a critical role in how they perceive themselves and sometimes it seems easier to criticize and pick apart every little flaw that you may see in the mirror. Rather than doing this, encourage your teens to be kind to themselves and avoid being overly harsh on themselves. Try telling them, "You would never say these cruel and unkind words to anyone else, so why is it okay to say them to yourself?" developing a healthy and positive inner monologue can be difficult because our minds automatically want to gravitate towards the negative as we notice the flaws first. But with the support of parents and open discussion about what teens may think of themselves, this is a great way to teach your children to put a positive spin on things and be more optimistic about how they perceive themselves in their environment. For example, reframe thoughts like, "I'm not capable of doing this," into something more positive like, "I'm going to try my best and learn from my mistakes."

People often underestimate how much our thoughts can affect our ability but by simply changing the way we think, we can have a more profound and positive impact on how we end up performing. Most of the time, a positive spin is met with reluctance. But try it for yourself and see how changing your mentality can have a direct correlation to how you end up performing.

Ultimately, it really lies within the parent to teach their child to love themselves for who they are and not tie their worth to the number of followers they may have on Instagram or if they fit into that smaller size of jeans. Building self-worth on a healthy foundation is the key to its sustainability. Emphasize the important values like kindness, compassion, empathy and respect for others as the primary benchmarks for a person's self-worth.

BREAKING STEREOTYPES

*J*ust like how there are a number of hobbies or interests that have been deemed "too girly" for men, the same can be said for women where their abilities are severely underestimated for certain activities and thus deemed unable to perform at the same standard of males. Not only is this false and an incredibly problematic generalization, it also severely limits the capabilities of both males and females. These are great hobbies to encourage your teen girls to pursue that might seem "unconventional" but have great benefits for mental and physical health. Helping your teens build new skills redirects their focus from daily stressors like social media in a healthy and productive way.

1. Martial arts

Being able to verbally assert themselves or de-escalate a situation is a good starting point but sometimes your teen may be in a vulnerable spot where they will have to use physical force. Learning self-defence as a young teen is particularly helpful and can potentially save your daughter's life. Aside from this, being successful in martial arts requires a high level of discipline and focus. It encourages individuals to use their physicality and improve on them to grow stronger and keep your kids moving and active.

2. Fishing

Fishing is great way to explore the outdoors and experience nature in an all-encompassing way. Many people choose to hike to their fishing spot which can greatly help destress and relax them. Being out in the open of nature can be an incredible distraction from the stressors of daily life. This hobby is certainly not encouraged enough in young teens, especially girls. Fishing encourages individuals to familiarize themselves with local flora and fauna and get used to being out in the wilderness for fresh air, rather than being cooped up indoors.

3. Poker

Poker is a great way to boost your teen's concentration and observation skills. It encourages self-control as you ensure you are focused on your own hand and has a number of cognitive benefits as it boosts mathematical skills and further develops logical thinking skills. It is an inclusive game yet is often treated as a game solely for males.

4. Woodworking

This is another hobby that encourages perseverance and focus on creating a final product. It helps teens develop their find motor skills and tactile side to create a project that they are proud of. If your child finds that they do not enjoy painting or pottery, consider enrolling them in woodworking activities to experience another activity that encourages creative thinking. It can be an extremely validating for your teen to be able to say that they have made something by themselves.

5. Golf

Golf is often regarded as a male sport because it can be quite male dominated. But for a teen girl, this is a great sport that is challenging to master as it encourages bettering your own game. It relies on the individual developing their own skillset in order to do better than they last did and can be a calming and relaxing activity.

6. Chess

Chess is a game that challenges a person's ability to think logically and plan ahead. It teaches teens the basics of strategy by employing their observational and planning skills for them to make their move. These skills are also transferrable as they can be applied to life situations and social encounters.

7. Survival camp

These are a great summer experience for your teens to experience. Learning survival skills out in nature will teach teens lifelong skills that they otherwise will never be exposed to and in a controlled environment with instructors and peers. This is a good way to push the limits and test your teens' abilities against extreme adversity, alongside teamwork.

8. Music production

Get your teens to tap into their musical side and tie it in with their technological knowledge to express them-selves by creating music. Music has a number of bene-fits to destress and help improve memory and mood.

9. Coding

For a long time, coding was very much a male-dominated field and still continues to be in many ways. The gender gap does exist when it comes to coding. However, for teen girls, fostering this interest in technology and computer science can open up a number of pathways for them career-wise. Computer science is an important field that is rapidly expanding yet not enough girls are being encouraged to pursue it as a career. Foster this interest from a young age.

10. Fencing

This sport teaches teens the dynamics of offense and defense while increasing coordination and agility. It is another great way to promote cardiovascular health as fencing, while it may seem deceivingly simply, is a full body workout that requires endurance and flexibility.

Ultimately, the possibilities for your teens to pursue are endless, regardless of whether they are male or female. As a parent, it is crucial to rid ourselves of these notions that certain hobbies are "too manly" or "too feminine" for boys and girls. Rather than placing these limitations on teens, encourage them to pursue their interests wholeheartedly and dedicatedly. By doing so, you open them up to a world of endless possibilities that teaches them that there are no limits to what they can achieve.

PLEASE LEAVE A 1-CLICK REVIEW!

I hope you enjoyed reading this book!

If you haven't done so yet, I would be incredibly thankful if you could take 60 seconds to write a brief review on Amazon or the platform of purchase , even if it's just a few sentences!

Your feedback will be a huge help in helping other readers benefit from the information in the book.

You can also contact us by sending an email to tcecpublishing@outlook.com

Like us on https://www.facebook.com/tcecpublishing/

Join our Facebookpagehttps://www.facebook.com/groups/397683731371863/ to stay updated on our next releases!

See you there!

CONCLUSION

While there are inherent biological differences between males and females, raising them really lies in the hands of parents to present them with all of the opportunity that they can, regardless of their gender. While society may insist on enforcing these strict gender norms, as the parent, you certainly do not have to and can instead choose to view your child as the unique individual that they are and foster their own personal preferences, hobbies and interests.

Always keep in mid to respect your children and their rights. Respecting their identity and evolution as they try to find themselves in this complex world can be a daunting thing for teens. It serves as another form of added stress, but when armed with the support of their parents, the encouragement can truly build their self-confidence and love that they feel towards themselves.

While teen girls face a different set of challenges compared to teen boys, many of the techniques and methods of coping with this from a parent's point of view share an overlap and can be used interchangeably as there is no "one size fits all" approach to raising kids. Understand that every child is unique, and it is a responsibility of the parents to recognize what makes their child different and act on it, instead of forcing them to conform to the status quo. This can be incredibly dangerous and force your children to close themselves off from parents to the point where you will have no idea about what they may be going through.

The cardinal rule that has been reiterated constantly throughout this series of books is that unconditional love should be the backbone of parenting. You should be able to strike a balance through trial and error of the different techniques offered in this book to find one that best suits your child in order to foster their development as an authoritative figure while also maintaining a strong foundation and bond with your kids that allows them to feel comfortable with sharing what may be going on in their lives.

Striking this balance is possibly the greatest challenge of raising kids. While teens can present a new series of challenges and frustrations, it is still important to note that raising your kids through this new stage of life can be extremely validating and rewarding as you witness your children grow and mature into young adults who are trying to find their place in the world and make their own impact. As these books consistently discuss the difficulties parents face when raising their kids, it is so crucial to point out that raising children is an immense joy and a privilege that not all people get to experience, regardless of how desperately they may want to.

LIFE STRATEGIES FOR TEENAGERS

POSITIVE PARENTING, TIPS AND UNDERSTANDING TEENS FOR BETTER COMMUNICATION AND A HAPPY FAMILY

INTRODUCTION

The teenage years of any child can be difficult to get your head around - for both the parent and the child themselves [1]. The changes to their bodies, thoughts, motivations and emotions are complex, so it's important to make this transition in their lives as easy as possible.

See the transition of your child becoming a teenager like a caterpillar entering the cocoon of adulthood, these are the years where they will gradually develop into young adults. Though it sounds beautiful and a work of mother nature herself, it's not. These years can be hard for even the strongest-willed parents, and trust us, your teens will test you at any given moment.

Yes, they'll reach a point where it'll become the most embarrassing thing in the world to be seen out in public with you - even if you're on holiday and there's no chance they will see anybody they know. The teenage mind isn't exactly a pragmatic one and very few things remain meaningful to them - with their worlds revolving around friends, teenagers of the opposite sex and achieving independence. Coincidentally, this leaves you, as a parent, sidelined.

In the modern, digital world of today; always keep at your mind that technology is proving to be king. Devices are been prioritised over genuine emotional connections with family members and social status, particularly social media presence will likely mean more to them than doing homework. All the more reason why they need strong, effective, positive parenting. It's going to be a difficult road ahead, and you have many modern technological distractions to compete with but stick with this guide and you'll surely make it out the other side as a better, stronger-willed parent.

As if that wasn't already enough, that wasn't even the punchline. Though technology has developed so far that you have the internet easily accessible at the touch of your smart phone, you still have all the usual teenager problems to deal with - technology just makes them ten times more difficult, is all.

Teenagers will experience many things through the ages of thirteen and nineteen; in these seven teenage years, your child is going to experience everything from first hitting puberty, all the way up to deciding what career path they want to follow, looking at further education options.

The first change you'll probably notice is that your fun-loving, no-holding-back child will begin to transition into a more rounded person, and not necessarily in an entirely positive way. Often alternating between self-doubt to contrasting confidence - and in the modern world of today, there's a strong chance that this will be heavily influenced by 'Sarah' liking your son's selfie on Instagram or 'Georgie' saying your daughter's haircut looks weird. The opinions of their peers, particularly on the open network of Facebook for all their other friends/peers to see, will always impact their behaviour and mood. The teenage years are therefore some of the most fluid of the entire lives - especially now that technology is becoming the king. Sorry mum, your opinion on your daughter's hair won't matter, no matter how many times you attempt to tell her it's gorgeous.

The transitions experienced during their teenage years are not only difficult for the child themselves but are immensely confusing for you, the parent, too. You were so used to looking after them, being attentive and addressing their every need - now you're probably just trying to worm your way into their now very private lives in any way you can - whether it's listening in on their conversations about somebody's stream on TikTok or your son's fanaticism with some gamer on Twitch. They're things you have no idea about, but you'll desperately attempt to be a part of their lives by trying to grasp it. The fact is, your role is changing, so don't fight it.

Much like your child is transitioning from cared-for to independent teen, you're transitioning from teacher to coach. You're needed much less than you once were, and there's absolutely nothing unnatural about that, most teenagers are the same. Trust that the years you spent caring for your child more closely have prepared them for what's to come.

Trust that you've prepared them for every social media battle, every "Sarah's getting an iPhone for Christmas, can I have one?" and every "Louis' parents have Alexa, we don't". Trust that you've taught them what really counts in life, what's right and wrong and trust that they'll follow the right path - not just what they think is cool. Remember, you can only take them so far, your teenager has to do some legwork too.

If they haven't already, instil values, beliefs and princi-ples in them that will last a lifetime. Once applied, they can use them when you're not around - you're probably not around because they don't want you to be, so they need these values to fall back on.

In this book, we'll take a look at various aspects of the transition phase from child to teenager, and even look further into the future at adulthood. Though we would never recommend you intervene too much in your teenager's life (as it can be disruptive to them building a sense of independence) we would recommend that you enforce a strong sense of positive parenting. It's important your child knows who to turn to when they have gaps in their knowledge and it's even more important that they feel they can trust you for the more serious issues.

*I*n your role as a parent, your role during their teenage years is just as crucial as it's ever been, though it may now seem as though you're not as important as you once were. Though your teenager believes they don't need you at all, you should know that's far from the case. This is simply a phase in their life, they're only human and it's natural. Think back to when you were a teenager, you probably acted in a very similar way, so first hold the judgement!

They may be irritable, they may be unruly, they probably don't believe in things like Santa Claus or the Easter Bunny anymore, but that doesn't mean they're not the child they once were, they're just making a natural transition and deep down, they need your help. They need your help, even if they don't realise it themselves. Don't see your child as somebody that's hard to manage, simply see the opportunities you can give them to grow.

One parent told us the story of when she had overheard her thirteen year old son speaking of masturbation on the phone, it was obviously a very new concept to him and something he had most likely heard about at school - either in sex education lessons or in the playground. She told us that when she had that conversation, she suddenly felt a sense of panic, like she didn't have all the answers she needed to effectively deal with what he had just said on the phone. She believed he lost his innocence in that single mobile phone conversation, when in actual fact he was just a boy transitioning into a young man, developing all the usual habits and interests a teenager would.

Though you will find many well-rounded opinions on how to deal with these kinds of topics on teenagers on the internet, you have chosen the best way forward with our book. In this book, we'll show you that there's really no need to panic, and instead you just need to employ strategies in order to effectively assist your teenager with the transition phase - being the positive parent you're destined to be.

Shedding light on various aspects of being a teenager and how you can motivate and engage with your teenager to help them face and overcome their problems. Whether it's a mean Facebook post, a group chat on Whatsapp that your child wasn't invited to be a part of or not owning the latest, top of the range smart phone. Or you know, one of the conventional teenage problems, like girls.

See, the world we live in today is an ever-changing one, and things that are covered in this guide today may be obsolete by tomorrow, that's just the way things are in the modern, digital world of present. Since the dawn on time, parents have cared for their children in regards to all aspects of life, including welfare and prospects. This will never change - the only difference now is that there's a much bigger platform to observe your teenager on. Your scope for observation needs to be wider, but again, you should not worry yourself on these matters.

Rather than worrying, as that will get you nowhere, focus your attention on how you can best assist your child in becoming the person you want them to become and somebody who can be proud of themselves. Learn to be more understanding, do what you can do to be there for them, and more importantly, take on board the advice presented to you in this book. Find what works for you and your teenager and run with it. In the remainder of this chapter, we're going to look at various methods in motivating your child to ensure their development through their teenage years and puberty in particular, is healthy - even when they're surrounded by digital devices. On the subject of digital devices, is anybody else just about done with ringtones? Everybody put your phones on silent maybe we'll forget we ever had them in the first place!

GETTING INFORMATION

Not so much in the general sense of getting information, but rather your teenager should, if they haven't already, have an education on the emotional and physical changes they're experiencing during their teenage years [2]. Yes, they've probably had conversations in Science and Sex Education lessons, but there's only so much they can hear from 'Mr Bowerman', he's a qualified teacher, he's not a life coach. You need to ensure that your child feels they can turn to you to fill in the gaps of things they may be too embarrassed to ask a teacher about. When/if they do turn to you, you need to handle it in the most informative, sensitive way possible without betraying their trust, and if you ruin things at this point then they simply won't bring these issues to you again.

It's important they have a well-rounded education on these matters, as they need that self-awareness to know that what they're going through is perfectly normal and most certainly natural. It's also an opportunity for you to support your teenager, so you should look to assist in any way you can to maintain a strong bond with your child even when they go through the 'letting-go' phase.

These changes, though challenging, are perfectly normal occurrences for a teenager, and there's no need to go into any further detail with your teenager if they do not feel comfortable with it. As long as they know that, you've done your part. In the modern, digital age of today, you could tell them to research it on their digital devices, providing they use accurate, reliable websites for helpful information. Providing your teenager is safely, sensibly and effectively using the internet, there is no harm in them doing this. The internet is a vast library of information that is constantly being expanded upon, so they should definitely use it if it spares them some embarrassment. That said, encourage them to bring genuine concerns, particularly if it's about their health, straight to you.

One parent recited a time where her daughter had asked her about her breasts developing. She had said that her daughter had concerns they were 'growing' and she had to explain to her daughter that she was simply just ahead of her class on this and the other girls would catch up. Her daughter then went on to say that her and her friends had googled it and that's where she found out about surgically-enhanced breasts.

That was an entirely different conversation to be discussed.

We tell that story to show you that although the internet has a lot of useful information, it can also present issues around confidence and inferiority, where young girls may use the internet, see surgically-enhanced breasts and then go on to wonder why a woman has had surgery to make them bigger. This is why safe, monitored use of the internet is important.

Facial hair, pimples, pubic hair, periods and chest hair are all aspects of your child's teenager years that are sure to also come up in conversation at some point, just make sure you handle the situation sensitively and ensure they know it's perfectly normal. You're doing your part without getting involved in unnecessary, potentially-embarrassing detail.

Remember also that these changes may be the topic of at least one or two social media posts - where false/inaccurate information is distributed daily. So, don't be surprised if you need to correct a few statements, with things like "You don't grow pubic hair until you reach high school" appearing from time to time. Digital technologies are known for spreading information that sounds like it could be true but often isn't - so be careful about what your child is reading.

LEARNING FROM COUNSELLORS

Though you're the parent, the primary caregiver, that does not mean you're in this alone. You may not realise it, but you have a much wider support network of friends, family and other professionals involved with your child's development - all available with help and advice.

Remember that teachers, pastors, psychologists, friends, family members are on hand - as they've likely already experienced a lot of what you are experiencing with your teenager now. Turn to them for advice, support, but allow your child to as well. Ensure that your child knows they have a much wider network available to them. Their options aren't just their parents and their friends, there are professionals and other family members/friends they can reach out to as well. Offer that branch early to ensure they feel safe.

YOU MUST LEARN TO BE MORE UNDERSTANDING

Understanding the enormous pressures the teenagers face on a daily basis is one of the solutions to insubordination. As a parent, you should try to find out the problems your teenage children are facing and try to picture yourself in their shoes. Lessen your authoritarian posture to them and genuinely seek to know them.

Build a positive rapport by patiently listening to all the problems they bring up and try to find the answers together. Give them breathing room if they need it, and stop nagging about their clothes, uncompleted homework, unkept hair, cluttered rooms and unmade beds. Instead, model how you think they should act with your actions and speak less in your home. Actions always speak louder than words.

Listen keenly to know their fears and burdens and be a source of encouragement to them. Try to relate with their friends so that you would know where they go to, and what they do there. Don't try to be a "cool parent", because that will put them off. Instead, be kind and considerate to your child and their friends. This will give you the information you will need to know if they'll be safe.

Sometimes your child will fail to live up to your expectations, and that is okay. When that happens, do not make a scene by scolding them intensely. Make certain to find a suitable balance between enforcing your rules and giving your teen the room they need to grow and find out who they are themselves. If your teenager trusts you enough, you can help them with problems they have with their homework or with their personal life. If they don't want to discuss it with you, you have to ask yourself if you were in their shoes, would you want your parents to be involved with the situation? Be frank with your answer so that you can offer relevant solutions to their predicaments. Relax. Take the family out on a picnic once in a while and show your children you would always be there whenever they need a listening ear, guidance or a shoulder to lean or cry on. Play and exercise with them. Go to the cinemas, ball games, school play and public speaking presentations. Attend their school's awards day. Call them on the telephone every now and then and let them know they could count on you. Be very clear about your family values, habits and attitudes so that they would try to live up to your expectations. Make them realise that you want what is best for them, even if it seems rough sometimes. Let them know that even when they come short of your expectations, you still love them because you know they did their best and you are proud of them despite the poor outcome.

Don't manipulate them. Ensure you are genuine in all your dealings with them, so as not to give the wrong impression and end up driving them further away from you.

PUTTING IT INTO ACTION

Here's a scenario where the above examples on working with your teens could come into play:

Marissa walked into the kitchen after an afternoon at the grocery store. She finds her son, Todd, sitting at the kitchen table. He's already started working on his homework. She puts the groceries down and immediately turns to him to say something. This moment can go in two very different directions with one result leaving the teen both angry and upset. Which choice do you think will elicit the best reaction for both involved? "Hey honey," his mom states, while Todd continues to write out something on his piece of paper. "Hey," he mutters, not really bothering even to look up to make eye contact. "What are you working on?" she inquired, leaning back against the counter, still focusing her attention on her son. "Math," he replied, again, not bothering to look up after his response. "Do you need any help?" "No," he said. His voice is raised an octave higher at this response. "What do you have after that to study?" she asked. "English," he replied. "Then?" "I don't know," he said. This time he sounds a bit agitated. "Just look at me. You don't need to get hurt with me. I'm only trying to talk to you." "I'm not upset with you, but I'm trying to do my homework." She could hear him speaking in a tightlipped tone. She heaved a sigh and turned towards the groceries. "You better be done by supper," she said.

In the background, she could hear Todd mimicking her words. That's how one interaction could go, but let's see how the same situation could be handled a little bit differently. "Hey honey," his mom replies as she puts the groceries down on the counter. "How's your homework going?" "Fine," Todd says. He continues to look down as he writes information on the piece of paper. "What subject?" she asked. "Math," he answered back. "Do you need any help?" his mom inquires.

"Nope," he answers back. His tone is short but not quite agitated. She notices his demeanour and decides not to pry. "Let me know if you decide to change your mind." She turns back to the groceries and starts putting them away. "Supper will be ready in an hour." For a moment he's quiet before responding. "Thanks, Mom!"

Of the two scenarios, which one got the best response? Which one would you have done? The second scenario had Todd thanking his mother for offering her help and letting him know when supper would be, so in the end, neither one of them would walk away angry. It is completely about how you handle each situation that will ultimately give you a better relationship with your teenager.

Your free gift!

AS A WAY OF SAYING THANK YOU
FOR
PURCHASING THIS BOOK, I AM
OFFERING YOU A FREE GIFT AT THE
END OF THE BOOK

FREE

*W*hat is Depression? Statistics show that four out of every one hundred teenagers experience some sort of serious depression each year. It's particularly scary when you think about just how vulnerable young people are as it is, without even factoring depression into the mix. Teenage mental health is important, and its key that you're looking out for warning signs [3].

Again, this is likely a much scarier statistic than it once was due to the increase in social media and online activity in teenagers. At one point, social media and use of the internet was confined to the family computer, now however, that is much different. With the inclusion of smart phones in our daily lives and our increased dependency on having a 'likeable' or 'popular' online presence, depression is far more likely to become a societal norm. With peer pressure to own digital devices and maintain an online presence as well as the child not being particularly happy with what they may be witnessing on social media. There are many factors that could make the child feel uneasy.

Most individuals who experience a form of depression can be helped with treatment. The difference between depression and normal sadness is usually related to the strength of the feeling as well as the persistence of the feeling. Individuals who are depressed usually experience these strong feelings for weeks at a time (often times much longer) rather than just for a brief period of time.

Some common symptoms of depression include:

- Feeling sad all the time
- Frequent crying
- Feeling irritable or angry
- Withdrawing from family and friends
- Changes in eating and sleeping patterns
- Feeling worthless or guilty
- Lack of motivation or enthusiasm
- Fatigue - lack of energy
- Poor concentration
- Thoughts of suicide and death
- Feel like nothing good will ever happen

- No longer enjoying things that used to be fun

ADOLESCENT DEPRESSION VERSUS ADULT DEPRESSION:

Adolescent depression can be very different than depression in adults. In teens, it is more common for depression to present itself as irritability or anger.

Depressed teens may be hostile, easily frustrated and may have frequent, angry outbursts. In addition, teenagers experiencing depression may complain of physical ailments such as headaches or stomachaches. Further, teens who are depressed are highly sensitive to criticism due to their already low feelings of self worth. Watch for these signs, but also understand that these symptoms may happen for any reason during this challenging time, and you only need to worry about depression if it occurs for an extended period.

WHAT CAN HAPPEN IF DEPRESSION GOES UNTREATED?

If a teenager's depression goes untreated, any of the following behaviours could occur [4]:

- Problems in school - a drop in grades, poor attendance, or dropping out

- Running away - a cry for help as teens try to escape their feelings
- Substance abuse - teens may apply "self medication" or escape from their feelings
- Low self esteem - teens may have intense feeling of unworthiness
- Eating disorders - often signs of untreated depression
- Internet addiction - an escape from their real life that actually increases isolation.
- Self-injury - is a coping mechanism for teens and an effort to control the pain inside.
- Reckless behavior - engaging in dangerous behaviors because they have stopped caring.
- Violence - more often seen in teenage boys, self hatred is sometimes acted out
- Suicide - any thoughts, comments or behaviours should be taken very seriously. If your teen is talking about, writing about or making suicidal gestures you should seek professional help immediately.

WHAT TO DO IF YOU THINK YOUR TEENAGER IS DEPRESSED:

As is stated in the beginning of this book, depression is usually treatable and is treated through talk therapy, medication or a combination of the two. But you need to first be looking out for the signs, particularly those signs that may have been hidden from you, like social media for example.

If you suspect that your teenager may be depressed, you should try to talk to them about it in a very nurturing and non-judgmental way and let them know you are there to support them. It can be very powerful to validate their feelings and to just listen without trying to educate or lecture them. Hopefully, your teenager will feel a sense of relief that they are able to talk about what they are experiencing, however if they continue to deny that anything is wrong - don't take their word for it, continue to be weary of their feelings and actions and seek help if necessary. It may be too scary or embarrassing for your teen to admit something is really wrong, however, as the parent you know your child and you should trust your instincts. It is best to get a professional opinion if you are truly feeling like something is wrong.

Your teen's primary care doctor is qualified to do a depression screening and to rule out any other medical problems which may be causing the symptoms which they are exhibiting. If there is no medical cause, your doctor can refer you to a health specialist to help your teen through this time. Spoken therapy, or counseling, with a licensed therapist or psychologist can be very helpful in assisting individuals in understanding why they are depressed and in developing strategies for managing depressive feelings. I have worked with many, many teenagers who are able to fully manage their symptoms of depression through prayer and talk therapy. Depending on the circumstances of the depression, there can be noticeable results very quickly for both the teen and for those around them. It is important that teens find a therapist with whom they can connect with and open up to. Trust between them and their therapist is a significant key to successfully getting through depression and allowing the therapy sessions to make as big of an impact as possible. It is completely acceptable and appropriate for teens and parents to screen or interview a potential therapist to determine if the individual will be a good fit.

Rightful thinking is very important for people of all ages, old or young, male or female. The important thing is to remember what you're thinking about and why you're thinking about it. What you're thinking about needs to be the truth, needs to be morally right, lovely, admirable, excellent, something praiseworthy and something that can bring joy to your life.

Take Paul, for example, who was thinking about sports: For Paul, he wanted to be a great basketball player. He practised his layups for hours, dribbled until dawn, and tried to perfect his jump shot. Paul spent hours on the court, all in hopes to be the one that all the scouts were after. The problem was that while he had a passion for the sport, basketball didn't always love him. In many cases, he realised that his drive to be the best basketball player on his team was leaving him disappointed and unhappy. When others were praised for their talents, Paul would feel ashamed. He began to think less of himself and doubted his abilities. No matter how many times he was out there practising, he couldn't seem to find a way to be the very best.

One day, his therapist reminded him of a scripture about mediation. She urged him to try it, explaining that by meditating, he could open himself up to what his inner mind is telling him and that would help him see if being the best basketball player on the team is honestly as important as just enjoying the sport. It's alright to have a love for something, but that passion shouldn't overcome you to the point where you no longer enjoy it, and Paul took her advice. That night, he went home and explained to his parents what his plan was. He shut his bedroom door so he would be alone with his thoughts, and practised meditation the way his therapist taught him. He observed his thoughts, he listened to what was going on in his inner mind, and he breathed so well that the focus was only on what was important. Then, it came to him, just as he had hoped. He decided that all that really mattered was that he was happy, healthy, and still had the joy in his heart for the sport. Everything else paled in comparison to that. The meditation helped him with the feeling of a renewed hope. He also felt more lively than he had in a while. Rightful thinking worked for Paul, and it could work for your teen too. They can meditate on any part of the scriptures in line with whatever they have going on in their life, with this example being a possible starting point.

Sometimes, taking certain antidepressants can be effective in dealing with depression. Antidepressant medication helps the brain in releasing the neurotransmitters that aren't active when someone has clinical depression. Antidepressant medication doesn't always work the same for everyone, and parents should be aware that it will affect teenagers differently than it would with adults. As with all medication, there are risks and side effects present.

With your teenager's consent, consult a doctor about choosing the medication right for your teen. Encouraging exercise and social activity is also very helpful for teens who are experiencing depression. Many teens find art, journaling and drawing in addition to traditional athletics helpful when feeling depressed.

Provide your child with avenues to distract themselves

from the complicated feelings they may be feeling. Parents who are dealing with a depressed teen may feel very overwhelmed themselves, which can make this a scary and uncertain time. It is important that parents take care of themselves and tend to their own needs in addition to the needs of their teen. Parents should have their own support during this time if feeling over-whelmed, whether this is the support of a friend or family member, a life coach or their own therapist.

In addition, most parents find it helpful to educate themselves about what depression may feel like and the process their child is going through. This can be done through the internet, talking to a doctor or to their teen's therapist, or through educated readings about depression. It is also important for parents to not blame themselves or each other for their teenager's depression. Depression can be caused by many factors so it is unlikely that any one person or thing has caused the situation. Remember, the good news is that most teens are able to feel better through one of the interventions mentioned above, and learning about depression and it's treatments is the first step towards getting your teen the help they need.

HOW TO CURB NONCHALANT
BEHAVIOURS AMONG TEENS

*D*oes your teen constantly defy you? Refusing to do what you ask of them? Well, you're not alone. This is probably the sole aspect of parenthood that all parents share when their child is transitioning into a teenager [5] - a young adult who's possible struggling to accept themselves, sees their parents as the enemy and faces peer pressure at every turn. Regardless of the reason your teenager is acting out in this way during the transitional phase, you're likely sick and tired of putting up with their defiant behaviour and you're turning to this book for some answers.

The first thing to remember is that this is not out of the ordinary, every parent experiences it and some teens demonstrate their frustrations in a much stronger way than others. You also need to understand that your teenager may be hiding a lot of tension, particularly feelings, from you. These tensions and changes in their body will inevitably lead to frustration and nonchalant behaviour is naturally going to follow. There are many complexities in your child's development process that make this an unavoidable aspect of parenthood.

That said, it's also entirely possible that your teenager is particularly defiant and takes things to the extreme. It's possible that they consistently refuse to do what you want them to do. No matter what you ask or expect, your teenager defies you. They always resist your authority. Every day is a tug of war between you and your teen, always a struggle for power in the house. Just once, you'd like your teenager to do what you want them to do without questions and attitude.

One parent shared her son's story from when he was a teenager and the parent struggled to cope with his son's transition from childhood to teenager. Much like the teenager was struggling to come to terms with the transition process, his changing emotions and growing body, the parent was at a loss of how to deal with the frustration his son was feeling. From time to time, his son would reveal that he was struggling to cope and was constantly fearing failure academically due to the constant distractions of modern daily life. He said the peer pressure to say 'relevant' and 'active' on social media was becoming too much and causing him to act out. Many of his peers felt as though grades, assessments and exams weren't essential, or at least weren't being seen as particularly important.

As we mentioned earlier, technology has become king, particularly in the playground, and though we may not fully understand exactly what it is about modern technology that creates such a buzz for teenagers, but we do know that digital distractions can cause negative patterns of behaviour. In the anecdote, the father struggling to come to terms with his son's changing behaviour was all a bi-product of the negativity caused through overuse of digital technologies, particularly social media on the son's smart phone. Though technology is good for keeping us in the loop with news, current affairs and much more, it's about time that parents really understood the pitfalls of modern technology in this digital age - and maybe even take a stand against it.

But let's get back to how exactly we can deal with the situation at hand. Your teenager is acting out, he/she is stressed, defying your requests. What do you do? Well, you have a number of options available to you, however, as the parent, it's your job to find the best solution for your unique situation. But remember,you shouldn't force teenagers to do what you want them to, this may only lead to them resenting you, or maybe writing some really dark song about you when they hit the big time in the music business. There are many strategies available to you that you can use to manage defiant behavior. Here are somethings to keep in mind when dealing with your teen who just doesn't seem like they want to listen.

PICK YOUR BATTLES

The first rule of fight club, I mean young vs old club is that you need to learn when to pick your battles [6]. Remember that your teenager is probably raring to go and could easily sink their teeth into a heated argument at the drop of a hat. Quite frankly, teenagers can be savage. When provoked or put on the spot, they will go for the jugular. Be warned and know what you're getting yourself in for if you opt not to follow the advice set out in this subsection. A flurry of emotions has consumed their brain, they're not thinking straight, bear that in mind. This could be for many reasons, as we have discussed.

Whether it's because they're not accepting the way they look, they're worried about failing an exam or assessment or their simply just too focused on their social lives, if your teen is consistently defiant, then they're going to be defiant no matter what. That means that if you don't watch yourself, you could find yourself in constant battles with your teen over every little thing.

Not every battle, however, is worth fighting. If it's cold outside and your teen really doesn't want to wear a coat, maybe trying to get them to wear a coat isn't worth fighting over. Instead of battling with your teenager on it, let them learn their own lesson by sending them out shivering, they'll soon learn you were right and that they should take on board your advice more often. If you're going to go to war, choose the battles that matter. How do you do this? Before starting a conversation, ask yourself the following questions:

- Is this battle worth fighting?
- Is there a genuine, life-threatening or potentially harmful consequence of what may happen? If not, it may be worth reconsidering

RESPONDING CALMLY AND RESPECTFULLY

Yelling, screaming, nagging and lecturing are just some aspects of parenthood that initially appear normal; in theory, you'd think these aspects would work, but in actual fact, they do nothing [7]. These methods are tried and tested, to be ineffective. Showing disrespect, anger and arguing back only make your teen more defiant.

You may be annoyed that your teen seems to spend their life on social media, or all their spare time on Call of Duty, but that doesn't mean you have a case for a heated argument. Yes, you should apply effective parenting techniques to guide them into being more productive, but think about what the right and wrong methods to apply in that situation would be.

Rather than opt for a heated argument, as we have advised not to, instead adopt a more calm and respectful approach. Use a more inviting tone to address defiant, unruly or unproductive/negative behaviour and open your teenager's mind to something that would better occupy their time. This is all about finding a more positive way of encouraging your teenager to do something different, away from technology and away from potentially unruly peers at school. Sometimes, it's not about what you say, it's about how you say it. Especially at this point in your child's life, they will likely take everything personally, even your tone of voice, so keep that in mind.

See, some teenagers will actually get a kick out of simply just trying to cause trouble with their parents, especially if your teenager enjoys the spotlight from time to time. Refuse to get hooked on the drama they are so used to seeing on social media and in viral videos. Don't take the bait and maintain a positive, happy mindset. This way, you will have a much better chance of putting a stop to any potential tension that may be building, and more importantly, avoid arguments. Show your teenager the respect any other person in your life would deserve and that way, they'll never get under your skin again.

The fact of the matter is that you should really treat your teenager in the same way you would wish to be treated by them and anybody else around you, regardless of how nonchalant they are. Though it may be difficult at times, particularly if you're competing for their attention with the likes of Instagram filters and Snapchat stories, take the moral high ground. We whole-heartedly believe you can do it, but it's going to be hard. After all, you're in a fight for survival with a teenager growing up in the modern digital age of today where smart phones and social media are commonplace.

Eventually, regardless of the situation or the cause of the conflict between the two of you, your teenager will become tired of trying to argue with somebody who just won't fight back. Your social media addict and your virtual reality recluse all want the same kind of things when you peel back the layers - they're desperately fighting for independence, probably without the skills to actually do it. Let them make a mistake or two from time to time and know to approach every situation with a positive, open mind.

SET AND ENFORCE CONSEQUENCES FOR NONCOMPLIANCE

Before asking anything of your teenager, you must first determine the consequences for noncompliance.

A parent friend of ours once told us that they asked their teenage son to do the dishes. Being a teenager, he wasn't best pleased and chose to act out rather than just get on with the chore that had been asked of him. He acted out, yelled, stormed up to his room and went on his games console. The parent, having not set any particular boundaries or repercussions for noncompliance, he didn't know how to respond to his son's unwilling behaviour. He was puzzled as to how he should react, he told of the questions that spiralled around his head. "Should I have shouted?" he asked.

The situation the parent had found himself in was a bi-product of a failure to prepare for the worst case scenario - but a common scenario. What do you do when your child defies your request? Coming up with a punishment/consequence in the moment can be bad, or can just leave you speechless - meaning your child just gets away with their defiant behaviour altogether. The last thing you want to do is come up with a consequence when you're angry though, so avoid that situation and have a plan in place for when the inevitable situation arrives.

The consequence you settle on should be one that makes an impact but at the same time isn't detrimental to your teenager. You want them to realise the importance of their actions and how defiance in life isn't going to get them far in life, but you need to consider their feelings too. It's a very difficult, very careful balance.

Fortunately, there doesn't have to be a 'consequence' in the traditional sense of the word, sometimes the consequence comes naturally. If your child doesn't want to eat, then they go hungry. If your child doesn't want to do their homework, they face consequences at school from teachers. They may face detention, they may get a verbal warning from a teacher. You can rest easy knowing that your teenager will face a natural punishment.

That said, not all situations have a natural consequence attached to them, meaning you sometimes need to intervene. Deciding not to do the dishes should therefore mean you have a punishment in place to accommodate their decision to not do the dishes. If they make that choice, they must forfeit their time on their games console, tablet, mobile phone and/or social media activity. In today's digital age, this means a lot to them, so you know they will soon give in and just do the dishes next time the scenario plays out.

There may be times when it is unclear whether or not your teenager should face consequences for their actions. For this reason, we have devised a checklist of sorts. A consequence is appropriate when:

1. Defiance doesn't lead to a natural consequence - your intervention is therefore required.
2. Defiance leads to a consequence that isn't significant enough for your teen.
3. Defiance will lead to a situation that puts your teenager at risk of harm.

At the end of the day, your teenager should not be able to evade the consequences of noncompliance.

NEVER TAKE IT PERSONALLY

We know, it's easier said than done. In life, we tend to take any situation that threatens to spoil our happiness in a more personal way. It seems easy to think the world is against you, when in actual fact you've just been dealt a bad hand at that moment in time. It's because of this that people tend to respond in counter-productive ways which result in useless, unproductive power struggles that only serve to make the situation more tense.

If your teen is generally behaving in an unruly manner then their defiant behaviour isn't just a choice at this point, it's likely just a way of life. That said, the important thing to remember is that it's not about you, it's about them. Their defiance is not a result of them disliking you, because that is probably very far from the truth. Your teenager likely defies you and all the other figures of authority in their lives. It's just the way they are and it's perfectly natural for them to act out in this way, but it doesn't mean it should go without punishment.

This segment of the chapter is instead aimed at encouraging you not to take their behaviour personally, because it's not personal. That is just teenagers. Once you accept the way things are now, it gets so much easier, and you quickly learn there are much better ways of responding to their typical teenage behaviour than just scream and get emotional. It's all about being calm and effective.

One parent told of a time where their teenager had their eyes glued to their mobile phone. Social media had become a priority to her daughter and she was taking it personally because she assumed it was because her daughter didn't wish to speak to her mother. In actual fact, teenagers today just love technology and unfortunately fall under the hypnotic spell that social media has on many people. It's simply too hard for them to put their phones down, it's not personal.

PROVIDE CHOICES

As we have already discussed, it's perfectly normal for your teenager to want more independence, even if they aren't really ready for it. Defiant behaviour is therefore often a bi-product of their desperation to gain control and power over their lives and how they wish to live. Nobody, child, teenager or adult wishes to be controlled, there's something built within us that means we're programmed to seek freedom - it's natural.

Of course your teenager doesn't want to be told what to do, who does? Whatever your teenager wants, they will find a way of trying to make it happen, much like we all do in our adult lives. The only thing with a teenager trying to do this is that they aren't equipped with all the necessary tools to execute their plans effectively yet. They're still learning.

Your teenager will never understand this during this point in their lives though, and this is a huge source of conflict in many families. It's for this reason that teenagers are so defiant when it comes to figures of authority in their lives, parent, relative or teacher - whoever it may be. Nobody will stand in their way.

So, it's important to expect some form of resistance from your teenager. Whether it's a refusal to do the dishes or simply not living up to your expectations in a way that really disappoints you, like not getting their expected grades in class.

A way to lessen the resistance you get from your teenager is to allow them a bit more freedom, as scary as that may initially sound. Don't worry, because there is still a structure to follow regarding this. Rather than instructing them to do the dishes, you give them the choice of which chores they wish to do. They must do one/some, so let them decide. Give them the illusion of choice; providing a framework for them that also projects a sense of freedom - and gets them working for their allowance!

Allowing your teen to choose empowers your teen and increases the chances they'll follow through. This is because they own the choice. They're in control because they control the decision.

That said, not everything should be on the table for discussion. Sometimes, your teenager needs to follow the rules and get the job done that is asked of them. Where possible, try to follow this structure. Not only are their benefits for the positive development of your child, but you'll probably see that more jobs are done around the house, and who knows, you may even get to put your feet up and relax for a bit. After all, it's probably time for some kind of role reversal, you probably deserve a break!

PRAISE COMPLIANT BEHAVIOUR

Contrary to what you may believe, teenagers care a lot about what their parents think of them. Defiant teenagers receive much more criticism and almost always face disapproving looks than they do praise and recognition. It's probably justified, but imagine how it makes them feel.

They hear a lot about what they do wrong. Rarely do they hear what they've done right. They hear about their flaws, but not hear about their strengths. Even the most out-of-control teenager wants to be praised from time to time, it's human nature.

Where you believe it to be necessary, you should never be discouraged from giving praise to your teen for complaint behavior. Sometimes they just need a pat on the back for a job well done.

STRENGTHEN YOUR RELATIONSHIP WITH YOUR TEEN

It should go without saying that the stronger your relationship with your teenager, the greater the chances are that they'll positively respond to your guidance and instruction. If your teenager has a certain degree of respect for you then they will likely wish to gain your approval.

Of course, strengthening your relationship with your teenager is much harder than it sounds. As you know by now, teenagers are very complicated to 'manage'. But, if your teenager has respect for you and you share a healthy bond, they are more likely to genuinely care about what you think of them.

If you do have a strong bond with your teenager, don't expect them to be shouting it from the rooftops or posting about their love for you on social media, because it won't happen. Just rest easy knowing that your job as a parent is that bit easier going forward - you're less likely to run into acts of defiance.

USE 'BROKEN RECORD' TECHNIQUE

As we mentioned earlier, you should probably expect a little kickback from your teenager when you ask them to do something. That's why you might need to employ the 'Broken Record' technique. This will help you to avoid the disaster that is the power struggle and the inevitable stress and tension that usually follows.

It works by simply repeating yourself, repeat what you need to say over and over again, much like a broken record would. Regardless of what your teenager says, just carry on repeating yourself, using the exact same words over and over again. Same words, same volume, same tone. Stay calm and follow the technique for the best results. Your teenager will get bored eventually.

One parent once told a story of the time he employed the 'Broken Record' technique and his teenager actually responded by saying "Gosh, you sound like a broken record". He responded with "Yes, that was the plan!". It might be annoying, but they soon give up just to get you to be quiet. Everyone's a winner.

TAKE A TIME OUT

It's okay to call a time out if it means avoiding unnecessary drama, tension and saying the wrong thing. If it means you can avoid a power struggle with your defiant teenager, call a time out so both parties can calm down.

That said, don't leave the situation and allow the issue to die without first reaching a resolution of sorts. Revisit the issue in a calm way after the time out and you can discuss things without the tension that previously built up.

Give your unruly teenager some time to vent to their friends on social media, if that's what they feel like doing, or let them go on a shooting spree on Call of Duty, if they want to do that too. Whatever it is that they need to do to chill out, as long as it is within the realms of the law, allow them the freedom to do it. Only then can you sort your issues.

PUTTING IT INTO ACTION

Thomas was tired of coming home from work to find that his son Mark doesn't do anything from the minute he comes back from school until dinner time. Thomas wished to have a child that will do what his mother told him to do, but she was always complaining that Mark only wanted to play video games and argue with her.

One day, he decided that he was going to change things for the better. The only problem was that Thomas didn't really know how to get that done. He thought it'd be more comfortable, but it turned out he might just have to learn to pick his battles, just like his wife previously had to do.

Thomas walked into the bedroom to see that Mark was

sitting on his bed, a controller in his hand and his bedroom in a mess. "Hey, bud. How was school today?"

"Fine!" he responded. Mark continued to play, careful not to get his character killed in the game.

"That's good, but maybe next time you could elaborate more than just fine," His dad smirked as he continued to examine the state of the room. He shook his head, surprised that anyone would want to live that way.

"Your mom says she told you to clean your room". "I will," Mark said, never looking away from the screen.

"How about now?". "When I'm through playing," he replied.

"No...how about now?". "Ahhhh...man." Mark dropped his controller as his character died on the screen. "Look what you made me do. Dad, please get out of my room!".

At this point, Thomas could feel his blood boiling. "This is my house, and I am saying you must clean your room, so you clean your room". "Why do you need to nag? You sound like Mom. I'll do it in a minute." Mark tried to turn the game back on.

Thomas stepped in front of the TV. "No. You'll do it now," he stated, raising his voice a little louder than expected. "You're not being fair," Mark yelled. "It's my room, and if I like it dirty, then I like it dirty." Thomas glared at Mark. "Fine. You can live in your room then. Don't come out until it's clean."

He was mad with his son's defiant behaviour, so he slammed the door closed as he left. Things could have been simpler and not gotten so far out of hand if Thomas handled it a bit differently. A compromise could have been made in the form of a deal. Thomas could have offered that if Mark cleaned his room then he would have played a game with him.

The moral of the story is that it doesn't always hurt to find a compromise - sometimes it means you avoid a lot of unnecessary tension and drama that would usually leave both parties annoyed and frustrated.

Finding a happy medium can be positive and productive for everybody involved, it's important to remember that.

DON'T GIVE UP HOPE

*I*n life, you will hear wise proverb after wise proverb, ancient teaching after ancient teaching and just general life advice in bucket loads, if we're being frank. With that said, there's a message we believed you should certainly hear, relating to parenting, highlighting that just because the journey is difficult, it doesn't mean there isn't a rewarding light at the end of the tunnel.

A wise man once said, "We must accept finite disappointment, but never lose infinite hope".

Martha and Conner were certainly trying to follow this quote when it came to their fourteen year old son Tristan. Tristan used to be a sweet, viola-loving primary/middle school student who played on the soccer team. But when he got to high/secondary school, he pulled a complete 180 and dropped out of orchestra and soccer. Though it sounds drastic, this is pretty much commonplace for a teenager today - especially one who may be self-conscious and confused about who they are and what they want to be. Remember, it's a very difficult point in a young person's life.

Martha and Conner were unsure of what to do when their son was going through this transition. At first, it was small things, like doing chores hours after he was first asked to do them. But then his first report card came, and his parents were shocked to find he had C's in all of his classes. When he was younger, Tristan did all of his homework on time. How could he be so close to failing all of his classes? Martha asked him this very question, and was shocked when he told her that he "had more important things to do than homework". What could that mean?

Tristan's laziness started to affect everyone around him. He put off his chores and told his parents he'd do them later, but never finished cleaning. This left cleaning the house to his parents, both of which were already busy with full-time jobs. As he grew irritable and moody, his parents became frustrated. Again, as drastic and out of character as it may sound, was and still is today, commonplace. Conflict with parents due to severe transitions in personality, character and interests is bound to occur, what matters is how these situations are handled.

Neither of Tristan's parents wanted to accept that they were upset, and ended up taking out their frustrations on each other. One night, Martha prayed for a sign of hope that Tristan wasn't doomed to be unruly for the rest of his life. She prayed this every night and was going to give up hope herself when she got a call from a friend. Her friend also had an unruly teen and knew of Martha's situation. The friend told her about a counsellor at a learning centre who helped keep her son on track. But Martha was unsure; nothing she and Conner had tried worked. Would it really be worth it to seek a counsellor?

Many parents choose to go down this route when faced with an unruly teenager who experiences drastic personality changes and acts out because of it. The important thing here is to point out that seeking the help of a counsellor is perfectly natural and normal, there is certainly no shame in it.

Conner thought it was a good idea. They set up an appointment with Leah, the counsellor, and drove Tristan to the learning centre the very next day. When they dropped him off, they were nervous. Leah promised them that she'd be a good source of help. But they had yet to see her work in action. When they picked up Tristan from the learning centre, they discovered that all of his homework was done! Nothing changes, if nothing changes, right?

Leah had sat him down and worked through all the problems, one by one until he caved and did the work. This was great news! Martha and Conner were excited for their new, more positive son. There was one problem, however: when they got home, instead of doing his chores, Tristan went into his room to play video games. They may have gotten him to do his homework, but he still refused to do anything else. Some behaviours appeared to be sticking around for the long haul.

Martha called Leah and asked what went wrong. "I had to work really hard to get him to even start," Leah explained. "Tristan didn't do his work until I broke down each problem for him individually. He's a smart kid, but he just doesn't want to do anything!" Martha sighed. This was frustrating news. She and Leah decided that he should continue going to the learning centre, and Martha would try to work on him from home. Every day, she drove him to the learning centre. When she picked him up, she would try and talk him through doing his chores. Unfortunately, it never worked. Martha and Conner continued to pray for an answer to their son's irritating behaviour, to no avail. But God works in mysterious ways.

Three weeks after Tristan started going to the learning

centre, he had an assignment about Martin Luther King Jr. He learned about how MLK went through trouble and turmoil but never gave up, working as one of the most remarkable civil rights activists in American history. He spoke out against evil and fought for what he believed in, right up until his death. Tristan was stunned; how could one man do so much work and never give up? That night, Tristan talked to his parents about Dr King. He was amazed by how dedicated the activist was.

Tristan was so inspired by Dr King, he decided it was time for him to step up. When his mum asked him if he would clean up the dishes after dinner, not only did he answer yes, but he did it instantly. Amazing, right?

Tristan was finally starting to realise that if he wanted to do good things in life, he needed to stay positive and do good work. Martha and Conner were amazed by this turnaround, and their hearts swelled with pride. They were so glad they didn't give up hope on their son.

Situations like this need faith and hope to overcome them. When dealing with an unruly teen or a disrespectful student - do not give up. Hold on to hope. With patience and love (for your kid and yourself), you will succeed in turning that troubled teenager into a triumphant teenager!

As a parent, you cannot control every little thing your teenager is doing – nor should you want to do it. The teen years are a time when your child is becoming their own person, so they need to have some room to try things out, grow and separate slowly from you. However, as a parent, there are expectations you have of your teenager and things you will and won't allow and it is important that you are clear and consistent about these expectations.

Teens will always push the limits and test you if they know that you are sometimes not consistent. An example of this is Anita, a mother who told her two teens that they could not have friends in the house after school until she got home from work. Anita wanted her children to use this time for doing homework and was tired of coming home to a house full of teenagers who have eaten half the food she bought for the week.

However, the very next day she returned home from work looking to relax and start dinner and there were four other teenagers in the house.

Needless to say, Anita felt disrespected, disappointed and angry. Conflict between parent and teenager was brewing, a perfectly natural occurrence in a world of parenthood and coming-of-age, but that doesn't make it any less frustrating.

Her response was to yell when she walked in the door and told the other teens that they needed to go home. Her children protested repeatedly causing a "scene" in front of their friends which caused Anita to allow them to stay and told them "this was the last time". When it happened the next time, Anita decided that she was going to make it clear that this wasn't OK, and make sure the other teens left and that she did not give into her teen's arguments. When she was clear that they had to leave, her kids then told her that the other teenagers did not have rides home.

This exhausted and frustrated mother then piled the teens in her car and drove them each home to get them out of her house and make her point. When she got back home, she yelled at her children and told them that this was not allowed. Much to her surprise, the next week the same situation happens again. Why? Well, while Anita was telling everyone this behaviour was not allowed, she was actually reinforcing it by not issuing any consequences and then on top of it, driving all the kids home which they probably thought was great. So, what could she have done differently? She called her best friend who suggested to her to do the following:

1. The first suggestion was that she should tell her kids that if they wanted to have all their friends over, they would have to compensate her for all

the food and gas in order to deal with their friends. If she put a monetary value on the situation, her teens might be less likely to have people over because it cost money!

2. The second suggestion was that she should tell her kids that if it happens again, she will call the parents of the other teens and explain the situation to them. She will ask them to come pick up their own children. This would likely cause a lot of embarrassment to her children, which is always good leverage. The key is that Anita must follow through with what she says she will do if this happens again.

3. The third suggestion was that she should explore whether there is an adult she can have come to the house after school for a brief period to monitor her teen to make sure no one is coming over. Her teenagers will likely not enjoy this and will feel like there is a babysitter present and may decide it is better to just follow the rules and be home alone.

4. The fourth suggestion was that if this rule is broken again, Anita should look for the consequences that are really powerful for her teenagers and let them know upfront that they would be enforced for any further breaking of this important rule. Anita warned her children

> that if they broke this rule again that they
> would lose their phone and video game access
> for one week.

Again, the most important part is that she follows through with this consequence if she needs to despite the yelling, badgering and blaming that she may endure from her teenagers. If Anita was consistent, her teenagers would quickly have stopped testing her limits because they would have known that she is serious. Ultimately every one would live in a more peaceful environment where rules, consequences, figures of authority are clear, consistent and predictable.

PUTTING IT INTO ACTION

Curfews are something that all teenagers face and might inevitably hate. As a parent, you should utilise a curfew to give your child freedom, yet show them that you expect there to be boundaries. Curfews are an obvious thing that all teenagers should face, and if a curfew is broken, then there should be consequences that occur once they have disobeyed their set curfew.

For Robin, she didn't see a reason she should have to endure such a curfew. She was good in school, always getting straight A's, and a champion at swimming. She had everything going for her, including many universities/colleges that were already seeking her out. Not to mention, she was one that rarely missed a curfew and thought it was pretty lame that her parents would even invoke such timing for her.

When Robin became friends with Regina, she started to push the limits of when she was coming home. She was driving her parents to wonder how harsh they should be on enforcing the curfew rule. On Saturday nights they set the curfew for 10:00. They didn't think that it was unfair, but Robin began to push the boundaries a little more, mainly to see how lenient her parents might be.

It was going on midnight when Robin walked into the front door. She wasn't really sneaking in, and she didn't think her parents would care all that much. They knew where she was and who she was with, so there was no reason to believe they would make such a big deal about it. However, they were sitting on the living room couch the minute she turned the foyer lights on. She jumped when she saw them. "Oh hey," she said. "I didn't think you'd still be up."

Her dad looked at his watch. "Do you know what time it is?" he asked. Her mom was quick to put a hand on his arm, silently telling him that he shouldn't be quite so hard on her. Robin just laughed nervously. "Yeah, it's midnight, or at least that's what time the radio clock said in Regina's car. Why?".

"Your curfew is for 10:00 pm, did you forget that?" her dad asked. He raised his voice a little, catching Robin off guard. She was a typical teenager, but yet she didn't usually find reasons that her father would yell at her. "No, but you knew I was with Regina and the movie got out late, then we went to get pizza. What's the big deal?". Then her mother stepped forward, most likely wanting to calm the situation. "You don't miss curfew like this and we were worried about you. That's all. We are only just asking that you let us know if you're going to be late from now on".

"That's not it at all," her father interrupted. "You are not to be late because we set a curfew for a reason," he said. "If you're late again, then there will be consequences," he said. Robin's eyes raised. "Consequences? Like what?" she asked. "We will come to pick you up if Regina can't seem to tell time," he said. Robin was mortified that her father would say such a thing. She couldn't imagine either one of them embarrassing her to the point of picking her up off from her friend. A part of her was so sure that they didn't really mean it either, but she didn't know if she wanted to test them like that. She then went to bed feeling a little unsure of things but not thinking too much on it. The next night she went out with her again. This time it was a school night, so she was to be in no later than 10:00 pm. As the time inched closer, she knew they should start heading home, but she was still confident that her parents wouldn't embarrass her and it wasn't like she was going to stay out all night.

It was 10:15. Her parents knew she was going out for ice cream with Regina and sure enough, her father came into the restaurant to pick her up. She felt the embarrassment from the moment he walked up to the table, until the time she said goodbye and left the restaurant with her dad. The whole way home she talked about how ridiculous and unfair it was but all her father kept saying was that she was warned. The concept worked because she never missed curfew again.

So, in the scenario, her parents got their point across that actions have consequences, and they would follow through to make sure she understood that. However, maybe there would have been another option that would have also gotten the point across. How would you have handled it? Would you have followed through with the consequence? What kind of consequences would you offer up, so that it would be a little less embarrassing?

It's crucial that your teenager know that they have rules that needs to be followed, but you want to make sure that your teen isn't scared of you or what you'll do. What could have elicited a better response?

Of course, when taking into consideration the points brought forward in this chapter, you also need to think about everything your teenager is going through. Not only is your teenager likely feeling the frustrations involved with having conflict with their parents (you) but they are experiencing other severe changes in their lives. They may be feeling the effects of issues around a lack of self-awareness or acceptance, confused/mixed emotions around their happiness, frustrations over their social lives and many more complications. It isn't an easy time to be a teenager, especially in the modern, digital world of today.

Always keep that in mind; if it's not smart phones, video games or virtual reality then it's the traditional issues like social life, changing behaviours and unruly attitudes. It's all part of the fun…

TEENS AND TECHNOLOGY

*W*e know, we've already discussed technology extensively in this book already, with issues surrounding technology cropping up throughout the various topics we've already honed in on. But, quite frankly, technology today has a much more significant impact on your teenager's behaviour than it would have done ten years ago, or twenty years ago, and is wildly different from thirty years ago [8]. This is why technology deserves its own chapter.

Let's take your first trip to the shop as an example. Your parents likely gave you a very long, well-thought out speech, listing the many guidelines you needed to follow in order to stay safe. Stop at the traffic lights, wait for the green man, don't talk to strangers, follow the yellow brick road. Okay, maybe not the latter, but you get the gist.

Why, then, if we are so cautious about our child's first steps of independence in the real world, are we not even nearly as bothered about their first digital steps on the internet and beyond? It seems baffling that with the growing importance and dependence we have on technology today, that people still don't see that technology and the internet is just as dangerous as the big bad world.

Technology, as we have mentioned, is an ever-changing, ever-developing beast that grows in popularity, usage and accessibility with each day that passes by. Meaning, there are just so many people using internet-enabled digital devices that you can't just assume everybody is a good person. We hate to be the people to break it to you, but the chances are, at least one person you've either communicated with or seen in some form on the internet is likely to be doing something at least slightly illegal. It's weird if you don't come across a weirdo on the internet every now and then. That's why it's more important than ever that both you and your teenager stay safe when trawling the digital realms.

It's not only disingenuous people who have the potential to harm that you need to be careful of either, there are many threats on the internet that don't lead to physical harm - there's emotional scarring, and aspects of the internet that will hurt your purse strings too!

Many young people don't realise that what they see on the internet may not actually be true, not truly understanding the power and strength of sponsored posts and other such marketing ploys. Particularly relating to those where a reality television star from Love Island or other related programming like Jersey/Geordie Shore, is involved. Many teenagers don't learn to read between the lines until their later teenage years, this is especially the case on social media, where everything you see, on the face of it, appears genuine. As a parent, it can be very harmful for your purse strings if your child is asking for the latest bubble face scrub because Charlotte from Geordie Shore is using it on Instagram. Unfortunately, the teenager doesn't understand that Charlotte doesn't actually like the product, nor does she believe it works, she's just being paid to use it.

The mix of recent technological changes and the ways in which we and those with fame or power engage with social media, combined with normal adolescent developments mean that parenting today is incredibly difficult. Arguably, parenting has never been as difficult as it is today. So, keep in mind that it's hard, your teenagers are living in an age where 'role models' aren't exactly David B and KB anymore, role models are often reality television stars (who are paid an awful lot for not very much work, and often very little talent).

With all this said, there isn't a one-size-fits all guide to how to approach your teenager regarding technology, its ever-changing nature and social media, you instead need to navigate their digital journeys alongside them, as best as you can, without interfering. Piece of cake, right?

Here are some helpful tips and useful nuggets of information that you need to be aware of when it comes to technology:

1. Teenagers are typically absorbed by their social lives - this used to be demonstrated in your teenager nagging to go to their friend's house or go play in the woods. Now, this will be a combination of that and time spent on social media. So, expect to see your teenager's eyes glued to his/her phone almost every minute they're in the house.

Social media, though it seems pointless from your perspective, can actually do some good, we said some… From uploading photos to commenting on viral videos, social media acts as an extension to a real-world friendship, and there are benefits to this.

2. Changes in the brain during adolescence mean teenagers are typically stressed and sensitive in a way that no other age bracket is. This can be demonstrated by them posting a photograph on social media and they only get ten likes instead of twenty. Your teenager may take it personally, they may worry people are beginning to dislike them. This may make them agitated or even add to the mounting stress they are experiencing.

On the subject of uploading photographs and not getting the desired response they were expecting, this may lead to further doubts about their image and therefore could make issues around acceptance and self-love crop up. Social media can be dangerous too.

3. The internet is the perfect storm when it comes to the potential for awful experiences to brew. From snide comments to slut-shaming [9] and nude photo leaks, social media is not only a platform for young people to express themselves, it's a platform for hate-fuelled actions to occur. From a pissed friend to a scorned escort, when something goes wrong with the relationship, watch out, because that person is likely coming for your teenager on social media. And, they won't hold back.

4. You may find solace in discussing the model for a healthy relationship with digital devices and social media with your teenager. Some won't be interested, but it's important for them to be just as aware of the negatives of social media as they are the positives.

5. Highlight the importance of developing good perception and conversation skills. As we mentioned, many teenagers often don't fully acknowledge the power of reading between the lines and often aren't even aware of its very existence. Challenge your teenager to question what he/she sees and not accept everything at face value just because it's commonplace.

6. Build a framework with your teenager that ensures their online activity compliments their offline activity too. Help them to understand that they can't be a different, more confident person online if that isn't going to ultimately reflect on their real world behaviour. Not only can this be confusing for a teenager, it can also help their development.

7. Remind your teenager about the performative aspect of social media and digital device use. Explain why people appear to be happier on social media, when in reality, you have seen them cry many times. Explain why Josh has 4000 friends on Facebook but spends most of his time in his bedroom, hiding away from the real world and real people. Explain why people post pictures of their shopping sprees on the internet. Explain that people project a false version of reality on social media, or at least a lot of people do.

8. With so many social media platforms in existence today, from the 'traditional' Facebook, Twitter and Instagram to the now hugely-popular Tik Tok and Twitch. Social media and content platforms are growing in number and popularity simultaneously, quite frankly it's weird if a teenager doesn't have an online presence today [10]. That said, they're bound to have at least a few followers, or 'friends'. It's important to remind your child that these followers/friends have no reflection on the real life connections they have made with people on a personal, face-to-face basis. Unfortunately, many teenagers believe digital friends are more important, when actually they should be an afterthought.

9. It may be an idea to invite your teenager's friends around to your house. Okay, don't try to be the 'cool' parent, cracking jokes and making your teenager feel embarrassed. Just show them that you're an under-standing parent who wants them to be happy and spend time with their friends.

Invite them to the house, get to know them a bit better and ensure your teenager knows that the support network they have in that house at that very moment is the only support network they really need. Anything else is just a nice little bonus.

Graham did this with his son, David. David had been spending far too much time on social media, making friends with other teenagers from different parts of the world who he had gamed with on Xbox Live, playing Fortnite. Graham was concerned that David was forget-ting who was in his real support network and chose to remind him in a very real way. He threw a small gathering of friends for David, they all watched TV, ate snacks, played on games and had a good time.

Graham said it reminded David who he really was and who he could turn to when times were tough. David described it as an eye-opener.

10. Ensure that both you and your teenager understand that technology and social media is developing at an unusually fast pace and that nobody really knows where it will be in five years. How technology, the internet and social media will look in ten years would be a complete stab in the dark. Truly, nobody knows. It's for that reason that we need to understand the beast we have mounted in the best way we can before we fully utilise its features.

Things are constantly changing, new threats are introduced with each day that goes by and both parent and teenager need to ensure the safety of each other when using internet enabled devices.

Not only that, but in a few years time it might not be too far out of the realms of possibility for digital devices to enable teleportation - it sounds crazy but technology is advancing so fast. Whether it's through our social media platforms, our emailing systems, virtual reality, or even the way in which we use the internet. Everything is changing, everyday, and if there's something new, you need to understand your child will find it.

LINDA STONE

Technology expert Linda Stone points out that continuous partial attention, or paying a little bit of attention to a lot of stimuli, mimics an ongoing state of crisis—breathing becomes more shallow and the mind hyper-alert. In large doses this behavior can make people feel overwhelmed, overstimulated, and powerless.

Teens are also learning to manage their time—an ability that takes a dip at ages 12-14. Helping them set goals and screen out distractions will help them control their own attention, complete tasks while preserving their energy, and stay in more conscious control of their focus.

PRIORITIZE OFFLINE CONNECTIONS

Young people need secure human relationships to anchor and guide them from infancy through adulthood. These interactions provide validation, information, structure, safety, love, and warmth. Yet both young people and adults say family members spend too much time online at the expense of in-person connections. Emotions expert Barbara Fredrickson believes that in-person relationships affect our physiology differently than online relationships do, increasing our health and ability to connect with others. Kids of all ages say they want parents to turn off devices and tune in to them. Consider enforcing rules like "no phone at the dinner table" or "no phone during homework time" to help your teen focus on schoolwork and family relationships. Likewise, most teens say they prefer face-to-face interactions. Though teens are trying to become autonomous, they also want to maintain close connections and to talk with their parents about things that really matter. They have been telling researchers so for decades.

BALANCE BREADTH AND FOCUS ON INTELLECTUAL DEVELOPMENT

Parents may find it easier to navigate the path of parenthood by taking in as much relevant information as possible about how brains develop so that the children, particularly teenagers are able to learn and emotionally grow independently.

Real-time play and real-life interactions are needed for children to explore, discover cause-and-effect, and lay the foundations of social skills, moral development, self-regulation, agency, and creativity. The skills that as adults, we take for granted on a day to day basis, without ever really taking into consideration just how beautiful the development process itself actually is. In the digital age of today, where social media, peer pressure, defiance and being unhappy in one's skin is commonplace - it's important to reflect on whether or not this affects your child's abilities to build on these foundations. Does it affect it? We're soon to find out.

For this reason, you should be wary of heavy Internet use across all aspects of childhood, but particularly the teenage years. It is much better to expose children to a variety of activities, but obviously this is easier said than done. See, social media particularly is especially detrimental when it comes to body image and confidence, as teenagers, particularly girls, are exposed to bikini-clad women with generally-unattainable figures. When a teenager is developing a sense of who they really are and what they can achieve, social media, among other platforms, can have potentially negative effects on those processes.

Now, this next part may appear complicated on the face of it, but hang in there. By the early teen years, the brain begins a process known as 'specialise'. Unused neurons are pruned for more efficient processing, and the number of connections between them increases. Teen thoughts becomes more abstract, integrated and logical; creativity and competency increases. Whatever teens are doing - from laying around on the couch to editing video projects for school - can become more firmly established in their brains at this time, which makes this a crucial period for learning and developing skills which may change their lives for the better.

For teens, we would suggest supporting their focus on their emerging interests - including online interests, while still encouraging reflection, analysis, creativity, spaciousness, a quiet mind, and quickness. The more tools, the better. This is a key point to highlight that we are not saying the internet is a bad tool in the development process, but heavy use can hinder development and negatively impact how your teen views themselves, others, and the world around them.

FOSTER EMOTIONAL AND ATTENTIONAL SELF-AWARENESS

Back to the biological side of things... Immaturity of the prefrontal cortex - the part of the brain mostly responsible for self-regulation and decision-making, can make it hard for teens to regulate their emotions and make good decisions. Peer influence, which can also impact good decision-making, is particularly potent between the ages of 12 and 14. Coincidentally, the early teen years are some of the most difficult for parents and the teenagers themselves when it comes to peer pressure. The desire to be popular between these ages can often outweigh common sense or even the morals that come with self-awareness and decency. The immaturity at this age means that for teenagers between the ages of 12 and 14, it can be particularly difficult to differentiate between what your teen actually wants to do, and what their peers are pushing them into.

But teens can be taught emotional skills, like how to take a 'meta-moment' – a pause between being triggered to do something and actually responding - to delay decision-making in order to choose a better path. This is especially important on social media where an impulsive act can have a wide reach and wider consequences. Think back ten or twenty years ago, without the consequences of the modern digital age, without the peer pressure that has become rife on social media, children may have been subjected to peer pressure, but it's nowhere near as harmful or impactful as it is today. Before the internet was as accessible as it is today, children could escape peer pressure by secluding themselves to the comfort of their homes. Now, the peer pressure follows. 'Meta Moment' is therefore crucial in today's modern world.

They can also learn to check in with themselves to become more aware of whether or not hanging out on social media makes them feel connected and happy, or sad and excluded. They can then choose either to maintain the feeling or do something to change it, if social media is not providing them with the connections that they deem necessary.

Take Malcolm, a young teen who spent most of his time posting photos on Instagram. He was a gifted photographer and gained a lot of likes and followers through his photography. Many people commented on his posts, complimenting him for his skill. But Malcolm felt like there was more he could be doing. Even though he had lots of online followers, he didn't really have lots of friends.

One day, Malcolm's art teacher told him about a photography contest held by a local college. He encouraged Malcolm to enter for it. Malcolm took the chance and entered some of his favourite photos into the contest. He won the second place.

During the contest, he made friends with other teen photographers. Many of them used Instagram for posting their pictures, but all expressed the same discontent with the lack of real friends they had online. The teens decided to exchange numbers so that they could communicate and share their work with each other, and make real friends in the process.

After this, Malcolm decided to leave Instagram. He had a good group of friends who would support his photography and critique his work when it is needed to be fixed. He wasn't getting social fulfilment from the application, but with an evaluation of his social media presence, he found a community that was better for his social life. Often, this is the case, and is something that we forget, even as adults. Often seen as a form of escapism where we can engage with our dreams, Instagram, and most other social media platforms are often substituted for actually engaging with that industry in real life. Whether it's because you don't accept yourself and don't believe others will, or you're just not confident enough to push into that real-world network of people, most of us fall into the trap of perusing 'communities' online over actually making connections.

Today's teens must also learn to focus and manage their attention on essential things, instead of being distracted by social media. Technology expert Linda Stone points out that continuous partial attention, or paying a little bit of attention to a lot of stimuli, mimics an ongoing state of crisis—breathing becomes more shallow and the mind hyper-alert. In large doses this behaviour can make people feel overwhelmed, overstimulated, and powerless.

Teens are also learning to manage their time—an ability that takes a dip at ages 12-14. Helping them set goals and screen out distractions will help them control their own attention, complete tasks while preserving their energy, and stay in more conscious control of their focus.

COMMUNICATION

*C*ommunication is likely the most universally-difficult aspect of life that appears to come so naturally but is so frustratingly hard to get right. Why? Because we all have different expectations when it comes to communication, and it's not just what comes out of your mouth that matters!

Adolescence is a particular time in life where not only is communication especially difficult and frustrating, but is also a time where you don't yet have all the skills necessary to be an effective communicator, or the desire to achieve it - at least not with their parents anyway.

Adolescence is a time of rapid change, not just for the young person but for the parents too. It might be hard to let go sometimes, but parents need to consider the following aspects of parenthood:

- A child's job is to grow up and become an independent adult. Think of it as if they're on a journey through adolescence, but unlike your journey however many decades ago, their journey is everything you experienced alongside the trials and tribulations of the modern, digital age [11]. As a parent, your responsibility is to help your child through the journey, when they need your help, much like your parents did for you as a teenager.

- Decisions can now be made together. Try to discuss issues to reach an outcome that you and your teenager can both accept. In the modern, digital age where your teenager is likely battling issues like peer pressure and self-acceptance, this is going to be much harder than you may realise, but it is possible with effective, clear and well-thought out communication.

Let's take a look at a case from 13 year old Kyle and his father Rufus.

Rufus worked from home, so was always able to keep a record of when his son was out of the home. If Kyle was ever late home from school, Rufus would know about it. One day, Kyle decided to approach the subject of staying out with his friends after school for an hour, rather than trying to go behind his back and lying to him about where he had actually been. Rufus thanked Kyle for bringing the subject to him, rather than using his own free will and going behind his father's back. Due to the mutual respect they had as father and son, Rufus granted Kyle's request, on the condition that he would be back each night before dinner. If Kyle ever missed dinner, Rufus would reassess the situation and there would likely be consequences. Kyle therefore knew not to cross the line, whether it be peer pressure, social media, or just being defiant. Kyle knew that acting out would mean his new-found freedom would be taken away from him - sometimes, that's all it takes.

- Young people may have viewpoints that are different from yours or may decide to explore activities that you don't understand. This is not to say that these activities are out of the ordinary or wrong in any way, but they may be vastly different from your interests. Try to see this as a good thing. They are learning to be their own person. Try to learn more about their interests so you can connect with them on their playing field.
- You will always feel responsible for your child's wellbeing and safety, no matter how old they are. Yes, even when they're in the forties

and complaining that they're finding grey hairs - at least its something you'll be able to relate to. When children reach their teenage years, they start to make their own decisions. Sometimes they make the wrong ones. You should feel slightly responsible, but remember, they're still developing but they're in the awkward phase of wanting independence too. Their wrong actions are predominantly theirs, always keep that in mind.

- Try to be supportive and not critical of them. They will, hopefully, learn valuable lessons from their mistakes. During this time of constant change, both parents and young people need to take time to care for themselves. You need to show you value your teenager, the person they are becoming and their uniqueness – show them your unconditional love.

Let's take a look at a case from 14 year old Shauna and her mother Vanessa. Vanessa was falling into the trap of constantly pointing out that Shauna was always on her mobile phone. Rather than celebrating and supporting Shauna, Vanessa was being overly critical - but she simply thought she was just being a good parent by trying to get her to come off social media. What she didn't realise was that for Shauna, using her mobile phone for social media was her form of escapism after school - she wasn't doing it because of peer pressure, nor was using it manifesting any kind of body issues. Shauna was simply escaping the stresses of school life.

Vanessa, rather than celebrating just how hard working Shauna was and praising her, was focusing too much on Shauna's use of her mobile phone, the one part of Shauna's day where she believed she could just kick back and chill out. Vanessa was being critical and this made Shauna feel as though her efforts weren't good enough and that she was a bad daughter for using social media. From this story, you can learn that there's a different way to approach getting teenagers away from their digital devices - show them there's something better to do, reward positive behaviour with an activity day that they would like - take them away from their mobile phone without them even realising that's what you're doing. Avoid situations of conflict and make sure your child gets the praise they deserve, and criticise only when it's vitally needed as a wake-up call.

GENERAL COMMUNICATION TIPS WITH TEENAGERS

The most important thing is to keep the lines of communication open. Tips include:

- Listen more than you speak: remember that we are all given two ears and one mouth. This is to remind us that we should spend twice as much time listening as talking. This is especially important when talking to teenagers, who may tell us more if we are silent long enough to give them the opportunity. It's so easy to forget that sometimes the best form of communication is to simply listen to what somebody else has to say. Sometimes, your ears come first, especially when it comes to teenagers. Not only to avoid situations of conflict, but to show your child that you value what they have to say and you care about who they are, their interests and love how God made them.

- Make time for each other together: Meaning, as the parent, you should designate time aside for your teenager, even if they're adamant they don't want to spend time with you - it shows you've thought about them. Teenagers are often busy with school, friends and other interests, but you can have a conversation with them over breakfast and dinner. Offer to take them to or pick them up from places; this will provide other opportunities for conversations. Make superb use of the time you have and build

strong connections with the minimal time that
you and your teen have together.

Take Stephan for example. An upsetting case of a child
who was emotionally neglected, as a teenager he struggled with his body image, representation of men and
therefore felt incomplete. He couldn't accept himself in
the way that God made him. His parents did not set
aside time for him, nor did they offer to drive him to his
friends house, in fact, they made little-to-no effort to
actually have an in-depth conversation about why he
was 'moody' - as they described him. Even if it's just a
chat before school over breakfast, put your phone down
for a minute and understand that work/your career can
wait a minute. Your teenager is more important.

- Give them privacy: Teenagers need their own
  space. For example, knock before you go into
  their room. Be prepared for them to want to be
  alone! In the modern digital age, you may not
  know what you'll catch them watching or doing
  otherwise, just a warning…
- Keep up with their interests: As we mentioned
  earlier, you should embrace your teen's
  interests, even if they are wildly different from
  your own. Try to listen to their music, watch
  their favourite television shows with them and

show up to their sports practise sessions. Your teen's preferences may not be yours, but making an effort to take an active interest in their life will make them feel loved. Not only will this help with their self-confidence but it will also help them to accept themselves and understand that even if their hobbies are unique/niche, they're just as special as any other teenager and there's nothing to be ashamed of - even if it's going trainspotting.

- Be a loving parent: Adolescence is a time when young people often struggle with their changing sense of identity and need to feel loved. Tell them often. Demonstrate your love using whatever physical contact they are comfortable with. Celebrate their achievements, forgive their mistakes, listen to them when they have a problem and show interest in how they plan to solve it. Support them in their problem-solving. Feeling included and special is vital for every young person's sense of positive self-esteem.

- Have fun: make time for leisure and laughter. Good feelings help to build good rapport and connection. Time away from the stresses of modern life is exactly what we all need from time to time - whether it's an escape from peer pressure at school or on social media, or it's a bit of time away from the computer at work. We all need a moment away from reality, nobody is strong enough to be completely resilient from the trials and tribulations of life.

NEGATIVE COMMUNICATION WITH TEENAGERS

Conflict is inevitable when people with very different viewpoints and experiences in life all live under the same roof, so the occasional clash with your teenager is normal and to be expected. However, ongoing conflict can undermine the relationship between a parent and a young person.

Negative communication is a common cause of prolonged conflict. Examples of negative communication include nagging, harsh criticism, or 'stand over' tactics such as yelling to force compliance.

It's not always easy to recognise negative communication. For example, well-meaning parents may criticise because they want their child to try harder. In the moment, you don't realise it - but you're actually making things worse.

You are using negative communication if:

- The conversation rapidly deteriorates into nagging, yelling or fighting
- You feel angry, upset, rejected, blamed or unloved
- The issue under dispute doesn't ever improve.

Take 15 year old Billy's story as an example. Conflict with his parents was arising so often that he truly believed he was the problem - not an easy achievement for a teenager, even if he wasn't entirely right in his judgement of the situation. It turned out that both he and his parents were using negative communication, which just made everybody unhappy. Not only did Billy feel unloved, his mother felt rejected - so neither of them were emotionally satisfied and his dad was so annoyed that he would often yell. Nobody was winning, as nobody was recognising their communication flaws.

Make sure you do your best to recognise these scenarios and find help to dissolve them if problems persist. Together, you and your teen can create a powerful friendship and bond that all stems from good communication and the ability to make use of the time you are together in your lives. Keep up with their interests, and include them in yours whenever they feel comfortable, but make sure to give them the time they need to make their own decisions and grow into their unique individual with values you have developed in them earlier.

PUTTING IT INTO ACTION

Edward was a hard-working man that rarely was home much to spend time with his wife and his son. On the rare occasion that he had, he tended to find himself angry with his son over his choices in TV and Music, mostly wanting to pull Charlie onto his side of thinking.

As a teenager, Charlie wanted nothing to do with that, but it always caused rifts in their relationship. One night when Edward walked into Charlie's room, he attempted to talk to his son, but his son's music was blaring on the speaker in his bedroom. Needless to say, good intentions seemed to fall a little bit flat, when Edward's old ways came crashing back in.

Edward cleared his throat, attempting to get Charlie's attention. Since the music was blaring so long, playing words that he couldn't even understand, the clearing of the throat went unheard.

"Could you turn that down?" he yelled over the beating of the music that was playing. Charlie stared at him, a blank look on his face. "Huh?" he hollered out. It was no wonder that Charlie couldn't comprehend what his father was saying, no one would be able to hear over the loud sound playing through the speakers.

"Turn it down!" he yelled again, this time making it a little louder, to the point where Charlie heard him. Charlie just laughed.

"It's how the kids play it nowadays," Charlie stated.

"I want to talk to you, and you can't even understand the words I'm saying," his father argued.

Charlie rolled his eyes and leaned over to turn down the music. "What do you want to talk about?" he asked. Edward was and remain at a loss for words as he didn't really have anything planned out. "You should stop listening to the music so loud. It'll hurt your ears."

Charlie laughed. "Good one Dad." He started to lean over to turn it back up, but Edward stopped him. "I'm serious. Give it a rest. Your mom and I aren't interested in hearing the music, and neither are the neighbours."

"You never are," Charlie mumbled. It was low enough that Edward didn't quite catch on to what it was.

"What'd you say?" he asked. "Nothing Dad," he said. "Can you please just leave? It's not like I'm hurting anyone." "You should be doing more beneficial things with your life, than listening to that…that…" he bit his tongue, letting the words fall off, but Charlie knew what he wanted to say. He rolled his eyes. "Just because it is not your cup of tea, doesn't mean it's all bad. It's not all about what you want."

"What's that supposed to mean?" Edward asked. Charlie heaved a sigh. "Nothing! Do you want anything else?" he asked, clearly annoyed. "No. Just keep it down." Edward turned to leave, and he heard Charlie say something, but by the time he was going to inquire what it was, Charlie had turned the music up. It wasn't quite as loud but loud enough. Edward shook his head and left the room. He would have another talk another day.

Edward obviously wasn't getting through to Charlie. He didn't agree with Charlie's choice of music for one, that was the first roadblock between them, but it only escalated from there. What could Edward have done to get a better response from his son? It's not about proving to your child that you're right and they are wrong, but communication is vital to any given relationship.

Let's see how Edward hands a new tactic and see if it gains better communication between the father and son. The music was blaring as Edward walked into Charlie's room. He walked over to the audio system and automatically turned it down a little, causing Charlie to show his sign of surprise. "What'd you do that for?" he asked.

"I need to talk to you and thought we could take a minute with a little less noise." The music was still playing, but the decrease was apparent. At first, Charlie didn't seem pleased, but he didn't argue. "Okay. What do you want to talk about?"

Edward motioned to the audio system. Charlie thought and figured that he was going to start yelling about how it was so loud, but Edward didn't do that. "Okay…" he stated. "Who's the band?" he asked. "Catfish And The Bottlemen, why?" he asked. Edward shrugged. "Just curious. It's a catchy tune." Charlie chuckled. "Really? You think so?" Edward nodded. "Can't much understand the words, but I'm guessing that's because I don't know the lyrics. Perhaps if I was familiar with them, then it would be different." "Uh yeah…perhaps," Charlie said. "Are they your favourite group?" Edward asked.

Charlie shrugged. "Pretty much I guess. I like the latest stuff they have out. You should hear it sometime. I think you'd like it."

Edward smiled. "Maybe I would." He dragged a chair and sat down, the music still playing in the background. "How's everything else going? School? Track? Oh, and your mom said you wanted to try out for wrestling. When's that?"

Charlie was beaming by this point. He immediately started to rattle off the information his dad asked, leading into the most in-depth conversation that they had had in a long time. Edward was glad he decided to go into Charlie's room.

Once communication started, it seemed to flood out of them, and that's sometimes all it takes. They were both left feeling good about the interaction, and no one had reason to argue or scream at one another. Good, honest, and open communication with your teen will help you form a bond that will only strengthen into adulthood. It's the impressionable years that you don't want to waste.

BUILDING GOOD CHARACTER

*R*emember when you were a teenager? You probably had to juggle school, family time, and maybe even a part-time job. Your parents probably did their best to ensure that you stayed out of trouble, and it's likely that they did a good \job of imparting some important life skills to you.

Now, you're a parent yourself, and you are faced with the problem of how to provide your teens with the life skills they need to face the future head on [12]. Not only that, but you're battling alongside the modern day stresses that the digital world has presented to us, in the form of social media and the widely accessible internet at your fingertips, presenting a whole host of issues from self-doubt and body issues, all the way up to peer pressure and rising conflict in the household.

You want to help your teenager build good character traits that benefit themselves and the people around them. You didn't know it then, but your parents were struggling with this same issue when you were younger. They made it through this troubling time, and you will too.

There are many things you can do to ensure that your teen is heading in the right direction. Let's take a look at just a few important traits your teen will need as a young adult, and talk about ways you can help your kids learn valuable lessons that will help them now and in years to come.

Independence

It is natural for teenagers to long for independence. Think back to your own teenage years - didn't you have a longing for freedom? Didn't you want to make your own decisions? Your kids are the same way. They want to make their own choices and they dream of leaving their mark on the world. It may be worth asking yourself how old you were when your parents gave you your first experience of independence, whether it was a bus journey into town with your friends or going to the cinema without them. Ask yourself if you were old enough or you felt you could have done with building on your maturity, this will help to inform you on how best to develop your teen's sense of independence and at what age to do it.

Fostering independence in your teenager is important. Even though you may worry about what your kids are doing when you're not around, you've got to let them gain that important sense of self-worth that comes from being trusted to be alone. They also need to learn the consequences, positive or negative, of their actions and how to handle them on their own. Be sure your teenagers know what is and isn't acceptable as activities. Never give them a reason to hide anything from you, and never make them feel that they can't come to you with problems. If they slip up, come up with a plan for dealing with the problem effectively — use negative incidents as tools for growth, instead of falling into despair. If you think about it, most of us have made mistakes!

Take Gina's situation. She was given her first opportunity for independence when her parents allowed her to take the bus into the city centre with her friends. One of her friends was caught shoplifting and though Gina didn't directly steal anything herself, she maintained the story that her friend was innocent - despite CCTV footage showing otherwise.

When Gina's parents found out, they were livid. They told Gina that no matter who it is, she should know the difference between right and wrong. Rather than telling her what to do next, Gina came to the conclusion herself. She apologised to her parents for lying and said she only did so because she thought her friend was going to be in serious trouble. She confirmed that she now knew it wasn't the right thing to do in the moment. Gina learnt the consequences of her negative actions so she could learn from that situation in case it ever arose again.

Don't let worry stand in the way of growth. Gina's parents didn't. Giving your kids a sense of independence doesn't mean that you're abandoning them, or turning them out into the world completely unprepared for reality. You can teach this life skill by gradually encouraging independent thinking, and by providing teens with opportunities to make the right choices. If you don't do this, you are doing your teen a disservice!

Your kids will become adults one day - and it will happen sooner than you think. Isn't it great to know that when you provide them with a sense of confident independence, you are also giving them a greater chance to be happy and successful in life?

Responsibility

Everyone has responsibilities. If your kids have no responsibilities now, then it is time to do them a favour, and give them something to be responsible for. Make the first responsibility you give your teenagers small ones. Perhaps it can be up to them to set the table for dinner, or to sort and fold their own laundry. Maybe they need to learn to make their own beds or pick up after themselves. Household chores are great ways to build responsibility and prepare your teen for when they're living on their own.

If they have already graduated from simple tasks like this, then they are ready for bigger responsibilities. They may be ready to start earning some money on their own. Perhaps they are ready to look for small business opportunities, or maybe they can be responsible for helping younger kids with their homework. If they're old enough, you might also consider teaching them how to drive a car. Being a responsible citizen is one of the most significant traits your teen can build. Make sure that greater amounts of responsibility are met with greater rewards, and be sure that the rewards are meaningful. Talk about positive and negative consequences, and be sure that your teen knows that he or she is ultimately responsible for things that happen in the future.

When Danny turned sixteen, he wanted nothing more

than to have a car of his own. He had already taken all of the driver's education courses he needed and was well on his way to getting his driver's license. However, his parents weren't sure he was responsible enough to have his own vehicle. Cars were a significant investment and could cause a lot of harm if owned by an irresponsible person. They told Danny he needed to prove his responsibility to them before they would consider getting him a car. Danny talked to his counsellor about it, and he suggested that Danny should tutor younger students in history. It was Danny's favourite subject, and he knew a lot about it. He was unsure about it, though, because he had never tutored anyone before. It was, after all, a considerable responsibility for him to take up! On the first day of tutoring, Danny was still unsure. He had two students asking about the Revolutionary War. He helped them study for their upcoming test by quizzing them about significant battles and important figures. The next week, the students came back and told him they passed their test with flying colours!

Danny was incredibly pleased and continued his work at the tutoring centre. His parents were happy too. He was helping out his community and sharing his knowledge with students! Danny proved to them that he was responsible, and they sat down with him to start the process of buying a car.

Making the Most of Relationships

If your teenager spends more time watching TV, or has their eyes glued to social media, or they just love playing video games more than they spend involved in meaningful activities that foster real-life relationships, then you may have the beginning of a problem on your hands. Of course, in the digital age of today, this is probably more likely to be the case than not, unfortunately, and is why you need to make the most of the relationship you have with your teenager, and the relationships he/she has with other people.

Kids who don't learn how to interact effectively with other people and shy away from opportunities tend to do poorly once they are out on their own. When you're so used to the interaction of a quick 'like' or a 'comment', it can be hard to be fluid when shifting between digital and real life correspondence, especially if you're still learning how to communicate.

One of the most important character traits for teenagers involves interpersonal interaction with people from various walks of life. You could encourage your teens to get involved with sports, or to participate in youth group activities sponsored by your church or community centre. Kids can learn a lot by shadowing adults at work, and they can even mentor smaller children once they have gained some experience. What matters most is that they are involved. Face to face interactions are crucial in their development into an adult. While it is true that computers and other electronics devices are here to stay, the need to interact with others in professional and social ways will never go away. Do all you can to be sure that your teens are learning how to create balanced relationships with other people. When it comes to intimate relationships, be sure to give your children the education they need, and to avoid being mislead.

Teens must know that attraction to others is a natural phenomenon to experience once they reach 12 and 13 years old. With TV and the internet, sometimes children begin experiencing attraction at an early age. This must be addressed at an early age so that positive under-standing can be modelled. If teens don't understand what's going on and lack the guidance to navigate this hard time, they may give into dangerous practices and unhealthy actions. When they deny it they become stronger, but if they give in to every desire of theirs, they become a slave of that desire.

If you are too close with someone of the opposite sex, it is like holding two polarised magnets together. How far can you hold two magnets together without it touching? It will always touch when you bring them close. If they are far away you can keep them apart but the closer you bring them together the attraction is very strong. This can be what happens when two teens are attracted to each other and have no guidance on how to deal with relationship.

It is important for teenagers to understand that intimacy is more than just physical contact. If you are not sure about how to approach this subject with your teens, you're not alone. This is one of those life skills for teenagers that can be tough to approach effectively! Luckily, there are many books and other

resources that can help you to provide your teenager with the skill and courage to follow the straight and narrow path to healthy relationships. Study these to learn how to effectively tackle these challenging subjects, as they are essential and can't be forgotten.`

PREPARING YOUR KIDS FOR LIFE IN THE REAL WORLD

Once your teenagers become adults, they will need to do all kinds of things from how to change a tyre on a car, all the way up to how to budget correctly when they move out and get their own place. They will need to be able to manage money effectively, and they will need to be able to make good decisions when it comes to things like buying a car, using debit cards, making decisions about who to spend their time with, and how to use that time most effectively.

One way you can encourage positive character traits and functional life skills is by modelling them yourself. Take a good look in the mirror: Are you the kind of person you would like your son or daughter to grow up to be? If not, you might want to take steps to become the individual you wish to and dream your teen will one day become. If you don't believe you're a good enough example of somebody your children can look up to, inform your children honestly and openly of how you could have done better - teach them the lessons they're going to need to know.

PUTTING IT INTO ACTION

Stacey was a bright student that always strived to do her best in school. Her mother, however, had become worried about her because it seemed like the only thing Stacey was interested in was studying and possibly reading in her spare time.

To many parents that might have been a dream come true for them, but to Veronica, she was still concerned about her daughter. Veronica was a single parent, having divorced Stacey's father when she was just a toddler. She had never been remarried and never went into another relationship after the divorce, as she really only had time to work and tend to her teen. Part of her wondered, if maybe Stacey had picked up on Veronica's lack of social circles because she never saw her daughter hanging out with many friends or doing anything beyond studying and reading.

She decided that she needed to take things into her own hands and that meant changing the way Stacey saw her mother interacting with those outside of their home. One day, Veronica decided to make it happen. Veronica walked into her daughter's bedroom, and Stacey had a book in hand, lying on her bed, while the book was propped up on her knees. She barely even noticed when her mother walked in until Veronica made a slight noise. Stacey looked up. "Hey," then went back to reading. "Reading anything interesting?" Veronica asked.

Stacey shrugged. "Reading a new book that Mrs Brewster introduced to us. It's pretty interesting."

Veronica, who knew much about what was going on with her daughter and school, knew that Mrs Brewster was her English teacher. "That's nice." She hesitated before adding the latter part. "I want you to come with me somewhere." Stacey looked up, obviously intrigued. "Where?" she asked. "I know a co-worker that has a daughter about your age. She invited us out for supper." Stacey groaned and started to make up a million excuses why she couldn't go. Veronica had heard them all, including the fact that she had said many of them too. However, she wasn't going to let Stacey out of this one. It would do them both a bit of a good. "It will only be a couple of hours out of the night. You can come back and read again another time. Just do this for me. Will you?"

Being a single parent, they had a pretty good relationship, so Stacey agreed, even though she knew in her mind she didn't want to do it. If it was going to make her mom happy, then she would. They left and went to the restaurant where Mallory and Megan already were. The minute they got there, Veronica worried that maybe she had moved too fast for Stacey. Megan was bubbly, outgoing, and the complete opposite of her daughter. Fifteen minutes in, though after they all had ordered what to eat and drink, it seemed like Stacey and Megan were getting along well. It relieved Veronica, giving her less and less time to worry and more time to talk to Mallory.

The dinner went well, showing Veronica that it was good for both of them. They decided to set up another time to get together, and even Megan and Stacey were talking about hanging out together sometime after school. When they got in the car, Stacey turned to her mom. "Thank you. That was fun," she said.

Veronica smiled and had to agree. It didn't hurt for her

to get out there and actually do something for a change that didn't include work. She even looked forward to going out again. So as stated earlier, evaluate yourself and see if

there are ways you can change to make things better on how your son or daughter interacts. If Stacey hadn't gone out to the restaurant, she would have still been stuck in her room, instead of finding new friends to add to her social network.

Present interactions can determine the future for you, and you should never shy away from that.

LIFE SKILLS THAT EVERY TEENAGER SHOULD LEARN

There are several skills in life that individuals should learn to help them manage the trials and challenges that they may experience while reaching for their dreams. For teenagers, these life skills will help them be more mature and independent. The skills will also promote good habits and responsibility. As parents, we play a crucial role in helping our children learn these skills.

MONEY MANAGEMENT SKILLS

Knowing how to budget and manage money is one of the most essential and challenging skills to master, so it is vital to help your child understand the basics of this from a young age. It may seem like a difficult task, especially when your teenager is already battling everything from peer pressure to body issues but it is achievable if you go about it the right way.

Parents should teach their children the proper way of budgeting their money so that they can have enough money to pay for their monthly expenses, as well as to save money to be used for special purposes or in case of an emergency. It is also important that parents educate their teenage son or daughter about the difference between wants and needs. One of the easiest ways to learn to budget is to have self-discipline on what items are necessary to have, and which ones would just be nice to have. By educating them in the difference between 'want' and 'need', you can guide them in the right direction.

Teenagers also need to know how to balance their checking accounts, set their financial priorities, and to pay bills. These are skills that can be grown over time in small steps. Giving them a clear insight of what the real world is all about is crucial in instilling them with a sense of importance regarding their finances.

Katherine gave her kids a weekly allowance in exchange for doing their chores. Whenever she paid them, her daughter Esther would go out and spend it all immediately. Esther wanted to save up money for the xbox X (it isn't even out yet, that's how eager she was) but kept spending her allowance on food and soft drinks. She would then complain when her mother told her she wouldn't pay for the system. Esther wanted the best of both worlds - and as adults, we know that can't always be the case.

Finally tired of telling her daughter no, Katherine sat her down and showed her daughter how she usually budgeted for the week. She divided up her paycheck so that every week she was putting money into her savings account. Then, she'd pay off her loans, debts, or credit card bills she had. With the money she had left she would prioritise buying food and basic supplies for the week. When she wanted to buy a nice, more expensive product, she would draw some money out of her savings account.

Esther decided to set up her own savings account and started to put away some of her allowance each week. It took a while, but she was able to buy the game system she wanted. She also learned essential values from her mother, that would later grow and help her develop a more fruitful life.

TIME MANAGEMENT SKILLS

Every teenager must learn how to use their time wisely so that they can accomplish more things. Time management enables teenagers to complete the tasks and responsibilities before the set deadlines. It also prevents them from experiencing stress and anxiety. Another benefit of time management is that it helps children make better decisions. Helping your teens with their time management skills will pay dividends for the rest of their lives, and is one of the most critical skills you can teach your growing young adult.

Parents can teach their teenage son or daughter how to properly manage their time by being a good role model and providing them the necessary tools to develop such skills. It would also help if they encourage teenagers to create a schedule of the things that they need to accomplish for the day and even for the week. They should also encourage their children to develop a routine.

Take the story of Natasha and her daughter Freya. Natasha always stressed the importance of having good time management skills by working her fingers to the bone to maintain a high level of efficiency. She would set reminders on her iPhone for everything. She would have Alexa give her reminders just in case anything went wrong with her iPhone. She had a routine for everything and always did things on time - it was exhausting, but it meant she got to teach her daughter efficiency, productivity and good time management skills.

Learning to develop routines can take a long period of

262 | LIFE STRATEGIES FOR TEENAGERS

time, but it can be incredibly rewarding. Not only can it motivate your teenager into behaving in the same way you do but it can also give them the kick they need to be productive, participate in activities and engage with the world around them.

Take Dave, who used to be incredibly unorganised and messy. His mom was often frustrated when he stayed up late the night before a project was due because he hadn't started it yet. He came home one afternoon and told her about an English paper he had to write. When she asked him when he was going to start, he shrugged. She decided to sit him down and outline the writing process so he could get it done before the due date. For the first week, it didn't work. But when the second week started, Dave found out there was a cool concert happening the day before the essay was due. His mother told him he could go if he got his paper done before the show.

Dave's essay was supposed to be five paragraphs, with quotes for evidence. He spent his first-day finding quotes and writing the introduction. The second day he wrote the next two paragraphs, and the third he wrote the last two. By sectioning out his time, he was able to get the paper done early and go out to the concert. He didn't like it at first, but once he realised there would be consequences for his actions, he started to schedule his time out.

Working with teens for an extended period of time has lots of value; if his mom hadn't kept encouraging him to manage his time, he wouldn't have grown positively.

HOUSEHOLD MANAGEMENT SKILLS

Teenagers should learn how to do household jobs such as cooking, doing the laundry, shopping for foods, and cleaning the house. If they are going to move out and live on their own one day, they need to learn these basic skills. Parents can start teaching their teenagers about these skills by assigning them with household chores that they can do for a week, starting small and gradually getting bigger as they gain experience and discipline.

One great way to do this is to have a family meal once a week where your teen helps cook dinner. Teens learn through practice and repetition. The more often they do something, the easier it will come to them. Not only that, but in the modern, digital age of today, it is so easy to implement - as anybody can follow the simple instruction of Alexa reading from a recipe from the internet.

If you involve your teenager in cooking dinner, they'll get better with time and learn a valuable life skill. As an added reward, you get to spend time with your teen and engage in great conversations. Aside from basic household skills, teenagers must also learn good hygiene skills and habits. They should be able to keep their bodies clean and their environment hygienic. Parents should educate their children about the importance of having a regular exercise schedule, eating healthy foods, and having enough sleep.

GOAL SETTING SKILLS

Teenagers must learn how to set goals and develop strategies to achieve them. It is important that parents advise their children to only set realistic goals. It would be better if they help them clarify specific goals and share some techniques on how to achieve them. Realistic goal setting pushes teens to better themselves and can help them increase their sense of self-worth and esteem. This is a time when social media is particularly harmful - as it can often set unrealistic expectations and goals for young people.

Brian was a busy student. He was the goalie for the football team, part of the school drama club, and spent time in the tutoring centre as he tried to improve his essay writing. His parents were proud of him, but sometimes it felt like he was going to exhaust himself! In his junior year, he wanted to be the lead in the school play and the captain of the soccer team. However, he also had a big essay assignment that was due the week of the fall play. Nora, Brian's mother, suggested he set more realistic goals. Instead of achieving all three, he needed to prioritise his activities.

Brian decided to start by setting the goal of getting at least a B+ on his essay. To do that, he scheduled appointments at the tutoring centre once a week. He then determine to try out for the school play, but for a part as one of the side characters. He could still have an important role that didn't require as much practice. Finally, twice a week, after soccer practice, he dedicated time to doing extra exercises. He knew that if he worked slowly, he could be made captain by his senior year!

PROBLEM SOLVING SKILLS

Every individual have their own problem. These problems can create a considerable impact on the lives of various individuals when not handled properly. In the modern, digital age of today, it's highly likely that your teenager is going to run into a whole hosts of problems from peer pressure to online bullying.

Teenagers need to learn how to think of possible solutions to different types of problems on their own. Teenagers with good problem solving skills can handle any problem that life has to offer. Teaching your teenagers how to deal with everything from interpersonal relationships to money management can be tough, but there are plenty of fantastic resources available to help you accomplish the task! So, think about the individual challenges you and your teenager face, and then get started. Each day that passes without action on your part brings your teen a day closer to adulthood. By ensuring that your teenager has the life skills he or she needs, you are helping to provide a better future.

Carla's son Logan usually came to her when he was struggling with something. They had a good relationship, so Carla was surprised when Logan came home from school and slammed the door to his bedroom. She knocked on the door and tried to ask him what was wrong, but he didn't answer. She gave him space in hopes he come and talk to her later.

At dinner, Logan explained that his friend John was mad at him but didn't tell why. John froze Logan out all day and didn't want to sit with him at lunch. Carla was sympathetic; this happened to her once or twice when she was his age. Carla asked him how he thought he would solve the problem. Logan wasn't sure. John refused to talk to him, so how could he know what was wrong?

Carla knew she couldn't do anything from home, so she suggested he ask a school counsellor for help. Logan agreed it would help; if he could have a mediated discussion with John, they could talk out the problem. At school, John and Logan sat down with a school counsellor. John finally admitted he was mad that Logan had aced his maths test, while John failed it again. Logan knew he was better at maths than John was, but didn't help his friend. Even though it wasn't actually his fault, Logan felt terrible. He decided that in order to resolve their issue, he would try and tutor John in maths. John was hesitant, but after seeing how much his friend cared about him, he agreed. This way, Logan was able to save his friendship and teach his friend the maths problem - solving skills he needed to pass.

It's safe to say that in the world we live in today, where everything around us is constantly changing, you need to teach your child a variety of vital skills that they will always need, regardless of technological advancements, so that they can survive.

Please Leave a 1-click Review!

Thank you for reading this book and engaging in the next step to establishing positive life strategies. I hope this book helped you in the same way it has helped many others.

I would really appreciate a short review for this book. Your help in spreading the word is greatly appreciated. Reviews from readers like you make a huge difference to helping new readers find helpful books like this one. I joyfully read every single review.

Just click on the link below and you will be taken straight to the review page on Amazon. Thank you!

<u>Review Book Here</u>

LAST WORD

The world we live in today, the digital world we have referenced throughout this book is a very complex world, a very toxic space too. Unfortunately, our children are about to inherit it from us, and who knows what it will become. See, the world today is changing at an alarming rate, being much different from how it was just five years ago, and completely unrecognisable from how it was just fifteen years ago. Technology is ever-changing and evolving, trends are becoming ever more materialistic and who knows what is to come after the digital age.

With all the uncertainty, and knowing just how difficult it must be to grow up in a world where your mobile phone isn't just a device, it's a lifeline, we need to approach things differently to how your parents may have done when you were a child. We need to own the situation we find ourselves in, upgrade our thinking, and re-connect with our heart and soul.

We have to apologise for our failings and ask for forgiveness as steps to heal the chasm between us. We need to model the behaviour that we expect from them. If we want them to tell the truth, then we must. If we want them to respect us, then we must treat them with respect as we guide them and set limits for them. Think of it like your teenager is on a tour bus in a foreign land and you're the tour guide - but the only thing is, the city you're describing is changing simultaneously as you're teaching your 'audience'. It's a difficult task made even harder by the ever-changing landscape of the modern, digital age where so many aspects of modern life can affect the development of your teenager.

If we want our teenagers to have compassion, then we must create the experience of compassion from ourselves to them. If we want them to understand us, then we need to understand them. Whatever we want and are asking from our teens, we need to be that. Our behaviour will be an influence for good to show them the way to move from adolescence into the maturity that adulthood needs to be.

Our teens need us to get off our phones and iPads, turn off the TV, the computer, and other distractive tech-nology and activities same with limit setting. Because, let's face it - sometimes we can be just as glued to our devices as our teenagers are!

We can't be a model for them when we are doing the same things we tell them not to do. "Do as I say not as I do" teaches lying, manipulation and deception It is time that we stop and smell the flowers. The world today is not what it was years ago, but we are still trying to educate and care for our children the way our parents did. They know more about the world than we will ever know.

There's no more room for lies or for excuses because they have seen it all, and many times they have lived through it. This is the time when we must try desperately to get close to them, to talk to them, to reach for them and make huge efforts to understand what they are going through every day. We must be patient, we must be ready to hear everything without being judg-mental, give them love and not punishment, they are already being punished by society itself.

It is our duty to make our homes a place of peace, a place where they can open up and speak of their pain, their problems, their doubts and fears. You and I have both sat before our children and heard stories of things that happened at school or anywhere else and they seem so wild and crazy that they do not register in our minds. We react negatively to their stories and call them liars.

But many of these stories and excuses are true and they live through them every day. The time has come to arm ourselves with patience and with tons and tons of love. It is time for us to serve our teenage children as anchors, as forts where they feel safe away from all the pain and suffering their world is made of.

Take the time to pray and speak with them a few minutes every day. Ask them about their day, how they feel, about school, or anything at all. The point is to work on opening communication channels. You need to learn about their interests. Watch their favourite shows, learn about their friends, and get involved with them. If you spend as little as ten to fifteen minutes every day just talking with your child, you are making an investment in giving them a better, safer life. They are the most precious parts of our lives, learn about them, watch them, share with them, soon they will be adults themselves and will go their own ways.

Now is the time to establish a true relationship with your teenager, not tomorrow, not next week, or not when you think they might want to talk. Actively seek to grow with your teenager and be the best 'tour guide' you can be. Don't wait until later on, as the opportunity will have passed and it is impossible to reverse time and the consequences of our not paying attention when attention was needed.

Think back to the stories of Gina, Stacey, Billy and Kyle. Our teenagers need our help, even if they don't like to admit it. Put your cap on, brave a smile and jump on that 'tour bus', because you're about to give the best performance of the parent/teenager journey through the modern digital age.

OTHER BOOKS YOU'LL LOVE!

CLICK ON THE BOOKS

Link to Book

Link to Book

Link to Book

Link to Book

Link to Book

Link to Book

Link to Book

Link to Book

Link to Book

Link to Book

Link to Book

Link to Book

Link to Book

Your free gift!

CLICK ON THE LINK
BELOW

**DOWNLOAD
YOUR FREE COPY
HERE**

REFERENCES

1. https://www2.ed.gov/parents/academic/help/
   adolescence/adolescence.pdf
2. https://kidshealth.org/en/parents/talk-about-
   puberty.html
3. https://www.youngpeopleshealth.org.uk/wp-
   content/uploads/2015/07/533_Mental-health-
   RU-Feb-2014-public.pdf
4. https://www.webmd.com/depression/guide/
   untreated-depression-effects#1
5. https://kuclinic.ku.edu/sites/kuclinic.ku.edu/
   files/files/Negative%20Behavior%
   5B1%5D%20copy.pdf
6. http://www.sdparent.org/web/site_2825_files/
   files/1381413101_Picking_Your_Battles_Prese
   ntation.pdf

7. https://childmind.org/article/tips-communicating-with-teen/

8. https://core.ac.uk/download/pdf/58825115.pdf

9. https://www.researchgate.net/publication/233217252_Slut-shaming_girl_power_and_'sexualisation'_Thinking_through_the_politics_of_the_international_SlutWalks_with_teen_girls

10. https://www.researchgate.net/publication/270161373_Teens_social_media_use_and_collective_action

11. https://www.researchgate.net/publication/324694265_PARENT_-_TEENAGER_COMMUNICATION_IN_THE_DIGITAL_ERA

12. https://parentandteen.com/building-character-in-teens-one-of-the-7-cs-of-resilience/

CPSIA information can be obtained
at www.ICGtesting.com
Printed in the USA
BVHW072236280121
599006BV00009B/790